The Networking Survival Guide

Get the Success You Want by Tapping into the People You Know

Diane C. Darling

McGraw-Hill

New York   Chicago   San Francisco   Lisbon
London   Madrid   Mexico City   Milan   New Delhi
San Juan   Seoul   Singapore   Sydney   Toronto

1 2 3 4 5 6 7 8 9 0   DOC/DOC   0 9 8 7 6 5 4 3

ISBN 0-07-140999-8

This publication is designed to provide accurate and authoritative information in regard to the subject matter covered. It is sold with the understanding that the publisher is not engaged in rendering legal, accounting, or other professional service. If legal advice or other expert assistance is required, the services of a competent professional person should be sought.

—From a declaration of principles jointly adopted by a committee of the American Bar Association and a committee of publishers.

McGraw-Hill books are available at special quantity discounts to use as premiums and sales promotions, or for use in corporate training programs. For more information, please write to the Director of Special Sales, Professional Publishing, McGraw-Hill, Two Penn Plaza, New York, NY 10121-2298. Or contact your local bookstore.

 This book is printed on recycled, acid-free paper containing a minimum of 50% recycled, de-inked fiber.

Library of Congress Cataloging-in-Publication Data

Darling, Diane.
   The networking survival guide : get the success you want by tapping into the people you know / by Diane Darling.
     p. cm.
Includes bibliographical references and index.
   ISBN 0-07-140999-8 (alk. paper)
   1. Career development   2. Business networks.   3. Social networks.
I. Title
   HF5381.D26 2003
   650.1′3—dc21
                                    2002156362

To Mom
Thank you for being my networking teacher. I
miss you and understand you more each day!

To Ilene Lang and Sharon Whiteley
Thank you for believing in me.

To Max,—the youngest man to send me a
handwritten note (at the age of 8)

Contents

Acknowledgments

Writing this book has been one of the most thrilling experiences of my life. For all my professors in college who know how much I hated doing a 10-page paper, there is no one more shocked than I.

Many thanks to everyone at McGraw-Hill who realized the value of networking and invited me to share my thoughts. A special thank you to Barry Neville who was patient with my nervousness as a first-time author, and to Pattie Amoroso for her conscientious editing.

Thank you to Joann Lublin for writing the *Journal* article and to Martha Donovan for networking us all together. Thank you to D.C. Denison, Diane Lewis, Davis Bushnell, Jeff Ousborne, Mickey Butts, and the team at XPLANE.

Tracing back the steps of how the book came to be is interesting. On December 4, 2001, I received a call from McGraw-Hill. That same day, *NBC Nightly News* called and filmed a presentation and the first thing that morning, I had been in the *Wall Street Journal*. Indeed, December 4 is a glorious day in my calendar.

Thanks to Mrs. Peterson, my high school English teacher in Greencastle, Indiana. I remember her teaching us about superfluous words. Her example was, "He had a smile on his face." She looked at us with a quizzical expression and said, "Where else would it be?"

Thanks to Dad for teaching me a great handshake.

Thanks to my wonderful board of advisors—Ilene Lang, Sharon Whiteley, Jennifer Potter-Brotman, and Henrietta Gates.

Thank you, Henrietta—my first investor!

Thanks to Jim Lapides at the International Poster Gallery, who gave me a cherished parking spot whenever I needed it during this project.

To Cody Traver and the team at CIO Global, who loaned me a computer when mine fried in the middle of the manuscript.

To Suzanne Rahall, who has been with me since the very beginning of my business, keeping my books clean and patiently teaching me how to read a P&L.

To everyone at Idealab where I have my office—Leslie Price, Hugh Shytle, and especially those with whom I share a printer who kept asking, "What are you printing, a book?" To the security staff who kept the building safe during all hours.

Thank you to Robyn, Bob, Julia, Max, Bob, and Barbara for including me in your family.

Thanks to my many friends and champions—Paige Arnoff-Fenn, Suzanne Bates, Ed Belove, Julia Carpenter, Pat Cauduro, Steve Coit, Roger and Margaret Darling, Amy Greene, Diane Johnston, Chris Joy, Susan Lapides, Trudy Lilly, Deb Rosenbloom, Shelly Rubera, Kristen Rupert, Susan Walker, and Peter Wilson.

Thanks to Dan for reminding me how much fun Hoosiers can be, teaching me discipline while writing this book, reconnecting me to my childhood, and much more.

Special thank you to my mom's friends who have stayed in touch with me since her passing. Your friendship and kindness have kept me going at times when it was very difficult. Thank you to Barbara Bennett, George Greer, Jackie Grubb, and Peggy Ouderkirk.

The only place where success comes before work is in the dictionary. ~ UNKNOWN

1

Introduction

Getting to know you
Getting to know all about you
Getting to like you
Getting to hope you like me
~ From The King and I, Rogers and Hammerstein

From your first conversation in the morning until your last conversation at night, you are networking. Many people don't realize they are networking when that is exactly what they are doing. If you have lunch with someone a few times a year to stay in touch, that's networking. If you participate on a board or community group, you are networking. If you recommend an attorney to your neighbor, you are networking.

- Have you ever recommended someone for a job?
- How did you get your biggest client?
- Is there someone you meet every so often for a cup of coffee?
- How did you find out about your favorite restaurant?
- How did you find that great vacation spot?

- Where did you find out about your apartment or house?
- Who do you call to raise money for your favorite charity?

Networking is the art of building and sustaining mutually beneficial relationships. There is a worthwhile reason for all parties to participate. It happens at home, at work, in our community, with everyone.

THERE ARE THREE TYPES OF PEOPLE— WHICH ONE ARE YOU?

It is said that there are three types of people in the world:

1. Those who make it happen
2. Those who watch it happen
3. Those who wonder what happened

Think of an inverted stoplight—do you make things go, do you proceed with caution, or do find yourself stopped dead in your tracks? Networked people make things happen, and they know others who do so as well. They are sought after as problem solvers and solution providers.

Which light are you? In this book we'll discuss how you can make things happen and teach yourself the networking tools and techniques that will make you successful.

WHY READ THIS BOOK?

I taught my first networking workshop to a nonprofit association that wanted to offer its members some tools and techniques to maximize their networking opportunities. While networking opportunities abound, the process isn't clear and is open to interpretation. That can cause some confusion and frustration. *The Networking Survival Guide* is designed to help make order out of chaos. It focuses on two facets of networking:

1. The outside, the practical, the skills, or the "how-to." These are aspects that can easily be learned with some training and practice.

2. The inside, spiritual, education. This is the connection we feel to others when we network and the possible reasons we may feel hesitant to do so.

Here are some comments and questions that I kept hearing. See if they resonate with you.

- When I meet someone, I don't know what to say.
- I feel as if I'm bothering people.
- If someone doesn't return my call in a week, do I call again?
- When I'm given someone's name, is it okay to use it?
- How often should I follow up?
- What method is best?
- How many times should I follow up?
- What organizations should I be a part of?
- Networking takes too much time.

Be easy on yourself. So far it's been the luck of your family, education, genes, and environment that determined your networking aptitude. Somehow you were expected to learn this essential lifelong skill from a variety of people and places without a curriculum or any structure.

Imagine about five or six people who all wear the same size shoe. They take off their right shoe, move one place to the right, and put on the right shoe of the person standing next to them. I bet the shoe feels a bit weird.

That is what this book will do for you and networking. You're going to learn and/or refine best practices and adapt them to your needs. Best practices are like new shoes: The more you wear them, the more they become made just for you. They protect what literally holds you up, they express your individuality, and they anchor you.

Summary: Getting to know people and letting others get to know you begins the cycle that empowers the networking process. Best practices make you feel confident, like your favorite shoes.

REASONS WE NETWORK

No man is an island, entire of itself; every man is a piece of the continent, a part of the main." ~ JOHN DONNE (1572–1631)

You need other people in your life, and they need you. It is unrealistic and impractical to do everything by yourself. You need others to help you get things done, both in business and personally. Why should someone help? Why are you asking?

When you know the right person to get a task accomplished, and he or she returns your phone call, you save

- Time
- Money
- Energy

Some of the common reasons that people network are

- Business development or sales
- Raising business capital
- Professional development
- Getting a job, assistance with career management, or a job transition
- Recruiting board members, management, or employees
- Fundraising for a nonprofit, such as a charity or an educational institution
- Social or personal reasons

This book is written from the business perspective, rather than the social or personal. Most of the examples will involve business professionals seeking to expand their network. These principles can also be applied to those who are seeking to network for any of the other reasons listed here. For example, you want to start a business and need working capital. You want to network to people who can help you. Or if you are job hunting, you want to expand your network to learn about companies and where you can make a contribution. If you are raising funds for a music camp, you want to find out who the alumni are and/or who loves music and would want to make a donation.

Whatever your reasons for networking, *The Networking Survival Guide* will help you determine the most effective techniques for your situation. Who is the best person to approach? What do you need to know? What is the best method? What are some strategies that will lead to your success?

When you get directions to someone's house, there are typically several ways to get to the destination. If there is construction, the path may change. Similarly, there are many ways in networking to arrive at your destination. The goal is to find a path that works for you. On occasions, try a new route.

Summary: Whatever the reason you are networking, it is a valuable lifelong skill. Get started, learn, and have fun!

NETWORKING CAN BE LEARNED

Every successful professional realizes at some point that he or she needs business training in order to reach the next level of his or her career. It is at this point that we begin to understand that we cannot do everything ourselves, and that indeed there may be some skills we need to develop.

When our company, Effective Networking, Inc., leads a workshop, typically people are a bit nervous at the beginning. They know that they are going to be doing things outside of their present comfort zone, such as introducing themselves to the group, doing some role-playing, and learning new skills.

Personal Networking — "Networking Is Crucial to Finding Stories"

Scott Kirsner, writer for *Fast Company*, the *Boston Globe*, *Wired*

For a reporter, networking is an essential skill to master. During the conversation with Scott, he mentioned that it is truly a mutual situation. It's crucial that he get the story as early as possible. He is also frequently being pitched. Here are some of his insights:

- Conferences are excellent venues.
- Ask questions. "Do you know where the keynote is? What are some of the cool gadgets you've seen?"
- Make notes on the back of business cards.
- Always carry business cards and a pen.
- Qualify a networking opportunity before you attend. Who will be there? What level in the organization are they?
- His pet peeve: Feeling worked on or having people flirt when they want to pitch a story.
- Keep networking—you learn by doing.

During a workshop, my first question often is, "Who loves to floss?" The facial expressions tell it all. They glance at the door and wonder how they can slip out. Often there are one or two oral hygiene fanatics who raise their hand and say they love to floss. Next I ask, "Who is competent at flossing?" Ah—the shoulders go down and the smiles appear.

Your dentist doesn't really care if you floss. They're *your* teeth, not the dentist's! But if you want to keep them, it's best to take care of them, even if it's a chore you really don't like. It's okay *not* to like it; you just have to be competent at it.

Lastly, I ask "who outsources flossing?" Usually that gets a laugh. I then point out that you can't outsource networking either. So you might as well learn to do it well.

Give yourself permission to learn networking and do it well, even if you don't love it. It's one of those skills—like typing—that you'll be really glad you took the time to get right.

Networking is like the express (HOV) lane on the highway. It works in a high occupancy mode, and it requires more than one person.

Those who are intellectually gifted value the "people" skills and know that they will help them get things done in life and accomplish the task more easily, more quickly, and with less hassle to all around them.

Summary: Be a lifelong learner and add networking to your portfolio of talents.

BENJAMIN FRANKLIN AND THE INTERNET

Each generation must transform the knowledge of the past into the promise of the future. ~ UNKNOWN

In 1727 Benjamin Franklin and other patriots formed a club for the purpose of "mutual improvement." The group so highly valued education that the club members were instrumental in starting the University of Pennsylvania. In his autobiography, Franklin writes, "I had form'd most of my genius acquaintance into a club for mutual improvement, we met on Friday evenings."[1]

Some of the questions required for membership were

- Do you sincerely declare that you love mankind in general, of whatever profession or religion?
- Do you love truth for truth's sake, and will you endeavour impartially to find and receive it yourself, and communicate it to others?[2]

Imagine what it would be like to meet each week with people of the caliber of Benjamin Franklin. The value of their intellects and viewpoints was so high that they wanted to learn from one another and share their knowledge.

In the 1700s, this group was obviously limited to those in the geographic area. We are now blessed with access to the entire world via the "Net." You can learn from others who are many miles away, and vice versa. The talent pool available to you has grown from your local neighborhood to a global one.

At first, many of those who embraced the Internet assumed that it would replace face-to-face interaction. While the Internet has facilitated communication in many regards, in-person time is still highly valued. When the economy shifted, the people who were able to survive and even thrive were the people who had a network in place and knew how to call upon it.

We are indeed blessed at this time to have *both* technology and face-to-face interaction as part of our networking repertoire. In this book you'll learn how to create your own "club of mutual improvement" and find ways to maximize your use of technology to enhance and manage your network for life.

Summary: We all want to belong. Find a group of people that share your interests and where you can be successful.

THE "PRESENT"

Yesterday's the past and tomorrow's the future. Today is a gift — which is why they call it the present. ~ BILL KEANE

The word *present* is extremely important in networking. It has multiple meanings, and all of them are relative to networking.

- To be successful in networking, you need to be *present*. You need to be in attendance. Some people say that they can multitask, but when challenged, many of these people retreat and admit that none of the projects (or people) are getting the attention they deserve. If you are speaking with someone in person, he or she is your priority. If this isn't the case, then cancel the meeting because you really aren't present. You are preoccupied.

- "My *present* information tells me that the outlook for next year is very strong." Your information is current. It is relative. It should be listened to by others. Be a news junkie!

- "I'd like to *present* the Ambassador of Spain." *Present* can also mean an introduction. You are facilitating a meeting between two people.

- Pre-sent—before you can be present, you need to do your preparation work. Then you can genuinely be present because you are familiar with the audience, organization, etc. "Pre" means before. Before you send yourself, know where you are going.

- Last but certainly not least, remember that the word *present* also means gift. When you are networking, you are a gift to that person and she or he to you! By solving the person's problem, you take away frustration and give her or him peace. You are a solution to the person's problem, and perhaps vice versa.

Summary: In order for networking to be worthwhile, you need to give as much as you take.

WHY THE OTHER PERSON SHOULD CARE

No person was ever honored for what he received. Honor has been the reward for what he gave. ~ CALVIN COOLIDGE

Everyone in the entire world listens to the same radio station—WII-FM. What's in it for me! You make time for others and they make time for you when there is some benefit for both parties. The payback doesn't have to be tangible; in fact, in many cases it is not. When you take the time to learn about someone else's livelihood and interests, you are more likely to get his or her time.

If it's not clear what's in it for the other person, then acknowledge that. Say, "I'm not sure what I can do for you; however, I want you to know that I appreciate your efforts and to let me know how I can help you."

People do not always expect cash compensation or immediate remuneration. In some cases, it's getting to know you and having someone appreciate his or her skills that merit a person's effort.

Listen to the challenges the other person is facing. When I was seeking funding to grow my business, I spoke with someone who could help. In the course of the conversation, she mentioned that she was looking for a contact at a specific organization in Dallas. I introduced her to someone who had connections there, and she was thrilled. I had called to get help from her and ended up giving help instead.

Summary: You have something to give everyone. It just takes a few questions to figure it out. If it's not immediately apparent, then stay connected to the quality of people you want in your life. Something good will come of it.

PERSONAL BRAND

Wherever you go, you represent more than just yourself. Years ago, when I was working in Europe, I had a colleague in the travel industry who commented on how difficult it must be for me to be an American. She explained that from her perspective the world looks to the United States to fix global problems and blames the United States when things go wrong. She was delighted to be from a smaller country, so that when people met her, they didn't expect so much from her country, and, indirectly, from her.

Companies create brands for each of their products. The messages associated with these brands convey to us reliability, value, and trust. We feel safe with brands we have known for years. For example, Ivory soap's claim of being 99.44 percent pure.

When you see someone walking down the street with a Starbucks cup, you automatically make assumptions about that person. It's the same with someone wearing Nike shoes or driving a VW bug. Brand is a combination of function and emotion. The product or service needs to meet our needs, but we also need to like it.

What builds or destroys a brand is reliability. It's frustrating if the product or service sometimes works and sometimes doesn't. Imagine what it would be like if your PDA decided to synchronize some of the data, but not quite all. After a while you wouldn't trust the product. The same is true with people. Unpredictable behavior is a quick killer of anyone's professional or personal success.

People have a brand, too. It's called reputation. Are you known as someone who gets things done? What do people say about how you work with others? Do you have a strong and accessible network? How do others perceive your temperament? These are things people decide after they have met and worked with you.

Your message to others starts much earlier. The way you dress, walk, wear your hair, and speak, whom you hang out with—all this affects your personal brand. If you are sincere, on time, and funny, then others get a positive feeling about you. It enhances your brand. If you are late, sarcastic, or interrupt, those you are dealing with will feel disrespected.

How much time do you have to make a first impression? It could be anywhere from as little as 3 seconds to as much as 20. One web site, www.first15seconds.com,[3] outlines what happens in 15 seconds:

- 4500 children are born.
- 6250 emails are sent.
- 187 business meetings conclude with no outcome.

What do you do with your first 15 seconds? Do you invest it or spend it? What can you do to create a positive personal brand? Brenda Smith is the managing partner of Prophet, a firm that helps clients manage their brands as a strategic asset. Her suggestions include the following:

- Recognize your personal strengths and gifts.
- Think about how you best connect with people.
- Consider what your target audience needs and wants.
- Identify the value you deliver to meet those needs and wants.
- Communicate in a way that reaches your constituents in their hearts and minds via the channels that work best for you and for them.
- Recognize the gaps in your personal brand.
- Invest time and energy to overcome those gaps.

When we purchase a product or service, we select it because we or someone we know has had a good experience with it in the past. We exchange our time and money based on our faith that the product will give us what we are looking for. When it meets or exceeds our expectations, we feel wise, wonderful, that we are "in the know," or that we have received good advice.

When you network, you are asking others to vouch for you. Your behavior reflects on them. If they recommend you for a job and you do well, they look great! If the project doesn't come in on time or on budget, it signals that maybe your standards are different from theirs and they won't consider one of your suggestions in the future.

Who is your brand manager? Who is looking after your reputation? Do you know how you come across? Products are easy to judge. People are buying them or not. If a product is flying off the shelf, then the manufacturer and the distributor can celebrate. If it is collecting dust, then they have a legitimate reason to be concerned.

People are the same. Either we meet someone else's expectations or we don't. How those expectations were created in the first place rests on our reputation and how we deal with others.

But you remember the product and that it has unique features. What are the results when you have a successful brand?

- You have improved self-confidence.
- You are in demand.

- You help others succeed.
- You know how you are different from your competitors.

Your brand also affects the bigger picture. When people meet you, they immediately put you in the same category as all the other people they have met in the past who are in the same group you are. That may be based on appearance, gender, profession (e.g., as Shakespeare put it, let's kill all the lawyers), country of origin, the company you work for, and much more. There isn't anything you can do about this, but you should be aware that it exists. If you had a bad experience at a certain store, that company's name remains blacklisted in your mind. If you meet someone who works for that company, you immediately think of this negative experience.

If you work for a company, remember that your behavior reflects on it as well as on you. Every day I walk through a complex in Boston that includes a Sheraton hotel. One time when I was walking in, I saw the bellman shaking his head as he looked into a taxi. As I got closer, I realized what was going on: The taxi driver was holding a $20 bill and trying to bribe the bellman to give his cab the next fare.

The bellman's decision not to accept the bribe and to give the fare to the next taxi made a statement about him, his company (Sheraton), bellmen, Bostonians, and men too!

Summary: Your conduct reflects on you and everyone in your life. Have self-respect and deference for others who you care about and who care about you.

YOU ARE A CEO

Every person reading this book is a CEO. Each day you make the same decisions a chief executive officer does. You determine where your money goes, you run interference when there is a dispute, you create short-term and long-term strategy, you add to your team (find a mate and/or have children), you relocate, and you decide where you want to go in life and how to get there. Even if you feel that you are not involved in making any decisions, you are choosing not to get involved. That's an executive decision on your part.

The CEO is the leader of a company, and you are the leader of your life. You make decisions about what to do and what not to do. As your skills develop, you can apply the same principles to networking. An executive's primary job is being the face of the company. You need to do that for You, Inc. Find opportunities, take calculated risks, and create a great team to help you get things done.

Summary: When a challenge presents itself, don't shy away from it. Take it as an opportunity to practice your CEO skills.

2

What Networking Is and What It Isn't

---

*Networks exist to foster self-help, to exchange information,
to change society, improve productivity and work life, and
to share resources. They are structured to transmit information in a way that is quicker, more high touch, and more
energy-efficient than any other process we know.* ~ JOHN
NAISBITT, *MEGATRENDS*

According to Merriam-Webster, *networking* as a noun did not
even exist until 1966. One can hypothesize that a network of people was not as necessary prior to that date, since people rarely moved
from their home community. Given that we had known most of those
people our entire lives, there was less to discover, as relationships
were handed down from generation to generation. Today nearly 20
percent of Americans move each year. Creating a new network in an
unfamiliar community can be taxing. The need to find a new school,
dry cleaner, plumber, and more can be exhausting. Not to mention
just learning how to get from one place to another. It's no surprise
that cars with the built-in GPS system are selling fast.

Now relationships must be started over each time we relocate and doing that is lots of work. Anyone who has ever moved knows that you don't just pick up the phone book and pick a school. You ask others to help you. Thus when you network, it reduces the stress of an already taxing situation.

Although Woody Allen says, "80 percent of life is showing up," it's important to remember the other 20 percent. You have to do something when you arrive.

Networking is being active. That's the *ing* part of the word. It requires your participation. Our network is the group of people who want us to be safe and secure—personally and professionally. It is those who are willing to lend a hand, share an idea, champion our efforts, and, when appropriate, challenge us to reach new heights.

Networking is

- Sharing of knowledge and contacts
- Getting the help you need when you need it from those from whom you need it
- Getting more done with less effort
- Building relationships *before* you need them
- Helping others

Most important, remember, networking is possible for anyone to learn!

I've talked about what networking is. Let's review what it isn't, so that there isn't any confusion. Networking is not

- Selling anything
- Getting a job
- Receiving a donation
- Securing funding

Summary: Networking is building relationships before you need them! Then when you need them, you know whom to call and he or she will want to help you.

MARKETING, NETWORKING, AND SELLING—WHAT'S THE DIFFERENCE?

Marketing, networking, and selling are interdependent, like gasoline, oil, and an automobile. The three components are more powerful together than apart. For clarity, the term *sales* can be used for non-profits and job interviewing as well. When you ask for a donation to your university or your cause, you are to a certain extent selling. You are asking someone to commit to an organization you believe in, and the request is that he or she make a contribution. Likewise, for a job hunter, when you secure the job, you sold your skills better than someone else and therefore secured the position.

Let's come up with some descriptions so that we understand what they are (see Figure 2-1).

- Marketing gets things started. It is an integrated campaign of promotion that includes web sites, advertising, public relations, and brochures designed to create awareness of your product or service. Marketing casts a wide net, educates a target audience, and creates awareness.

- Networking is the next step; it narrows the scope. It is people-driven, not company- or media-driven. It's personal. It

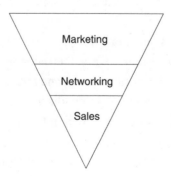

Figure 2-1 Marketing, Networking, and Sales

connects you to people who may want what you have, know others who do, or play a role in the decision. Networking is cost-effective.

- Selling connects the solution and the problem. By this time, the potential seller or buyer has been identified and the negotiation begins. It is the exchange of currency for a product or service. When networking and marketing have done their job, selling is much easier. You are speaking with a qualified customer.

It is tempting to skip the networking segment and go for the sale. If you are job hunting, you want to get straight to someone who can interview you. Similarly, if you are looking to recruit, you want to meet qualified candidates. There is a risk, however, that although you will spend time with interesting people, they may not be the people who can help you with your present problem. To maximize the hours of effort, networking is the best way to get to decision makers and those who influence them.

Here's an example. How many people do you know who have attended a networking event and walked out with a signed contract for business? Or walked out with a signed job offer, benefits negotiated, and references checked? (Assuming you wanted to work for that person sight unseen!)

Most of us would be properly cautious if those "too good to be true" situations happened. It's unwise to put the cart before the horse. The cart is likely to go astray, and the attached horse will get dragged along with it.

Selling is an art, and many people are very good at it. When we want to purchase something, we gather enough information so that we can make our decision, take action, and then move on. By the time we get to the "buy" stage, we have conducted due diligence and determined that we have enough information to make a proper decision.

Summary: It is tempting to rush through the process. Be patient.

DEFINITION OF NETWORKING VERSUS SCHMOOZING

You schmooze, you lose. ~ LENI CHAUVIN, FOUNDER OF
SUPERSTAR NETWORKING

Networking is sometimes confused with schmoozing. Schmoozing
has the connotation that you are getting something from someone with
no benefit to the other person. It's a take situation.

Going back to the dictionary, there are several definitions of
schmoozing and how it is about casual conversation. There is also a
definition, "to gain an advantage or make a social connection." That's
how most people feel when someone is schmoozing them. It's also
why many of us don't like to go to networking events. We don't want
to be part of that group. Those people often come across as social
climbers.

Conferences, trade shows, and other meetings often have "networking" time. I've never seen it advertised as "schmooze" time.

One of the biggest pet peeves I hear from people is that people
want something from them without even a *thought* of giving back.
After a bit of time, this can be quite frustrating and can wear out an
otherwise good relationship. We all can probably think of one or two
people that we rarely hear from unless they want something from us.

Networking is something that people talk about and know they
should do, but that they don't know how to get started doing. As when
computers are networked, the situation is clear—either the connection between the two works or it doesn't. Networking is an exchange
of information or services.

We have different people in our lives for different reasons. Some
of them help us to make money, some make us laugh, and others
stretch our minds. With some we share a hobby or interest. Many we
just like. A few we don't like, and they probably aren't crazy about
us either.

Time is limited, and we need to make difficult choices. Whom
do we make time for? Who makes time for us? Why?

The simple answer is

- We make time for people whom we like and who like us.
- We find time for people who make us feel positive, energized, and worthy.
- We take time for people to whom we can offer value.

What do we do with the rest? They belong in our "acquaintance" network. Rarely do we want to pursue a business relationship with them—only if there is no other option.

What creates that chemistry? What connects us? What can we do to attract positive and energetic people? What can we do to be one of those people? Simply reverse roles. What approach do you respond to? Why do you make time for some people and not others? You have the answers right now.

Summary: Be sincere and give back.

TYPES OF NETWORKING

In a nutshell, networking falls into two categories:

1. *Strategic*. This is planned. There is a specific person that you want to meet for a specific reason. You ask people who know both parties for an introduction.

2. *Serendipity*. This is an unplanned or chance encounter that leads to a mutually beneficial relationship.

In *The Networking Survival Guide* we'll discuss both; however, the focus will be on strategic networking. Why? Strategic networking has a stated purpose and therefore a desired outcome. By definition, there are results that we want and consequences if they do not materialize. We have in our mind what will go right, and also what could go wrong. We anticipate every sentence, body movement, action, and reaction. Therefore, we sometimes get nervous and anxious.

A chance encounter is just the opposite. Nothing is planned, so there are no expectations and there isn't any time to get nervous. When it's all over, we can sit back and take a deep breath. Often that is when it hits us what happened.

The word *serendipity* comes from the Persian fairy tale *The Three Princes of Serendip.* "They were always making discoveries, by accident and sagacity, of things which they were not in quest of."[4] It is now defined as, "the faculty or phenomenon of finding valuable or agreeable things not sought for."[5]

Strategic networking prepares us for the serendipitous moments. When we are confident of our ability to meet people and explore a mutually beneficial relationship, we are more likely to be open to chance encounters and convert them to mutually beneficial relationships.

Summary: When you are confident of your networking ability, you are most ready to be spontaneous.

STATISTICS

What experience are your clients having with the people in your company? We don't do business with a company, we do business with people, usually people that we like. If that relationship sours, the firm earns less money and people lose their jobs. People are the deciding factor. Either they make a contribution to the business or they are a drain. It all goes back to people. Look at these numbers:

- 15 percent of customers switch products to get a lower price.
- 15 percent find a better product.
- 70 percent leave because of the human interaction of doing business with that vendor.[6]

These numbers are quite telling. Hire people who both are well skilled in the tasks that need to get done and also have mastered the

"Welcome to My Dinner Party!"

Richard Saul Wurman, founder of TED (Technology, Entertainment & Design) and author of 80 books

Richard Saul Wurman sees patterns and likes to explore them. He defines patterns as "three things: numbers, ideas that reinforce each other, and ideas that don't."

Years ago he saw a pattern, and that was the alliance between technology, entertainment, and design. So he created a conference to bring the best minds together and share ideas. Thus the conference fondly known as TED was born.

He felt frustrated when he was traveling and would arrive at a new destination, look out the window to get his bearings, and still feel lost. The name of the street mattered less than what was on the street corner. Frustrated because guidebooks didn't help him, he created the Access Guides.

An interesting conversation is at the heart of a dinner party, and the same is true at his conferences. (He also runs TEDMED. "This is a conference about a business missing in the USA . . . the collection of media and technologies that enable individuals to seek and obtain a healthier life through the understanding of information.")

Wurman is a fan of serendipity. He loves a conversation and the uncertainty of where it will land. For him, that is what networking is all about. Here are some of his insights and thoughts on networking:

- Networking provides potential for greater joy.
- Discover common interests.
- Develop good friendships.
- Business gets done!
- Need to understand what people do.
- Be curious.
- Look at the dashboard—what does it tell you?
- Networking allows you to explore differences as well as what you have in common.
- Don't distance yourself from failure.
- People like to make things complicated.
- Break bread.
- What drives him is that he's always confident, and he's always terrified.

- The desire not to fail is the same as being shy.
- Be a good listener.
- Like interesting people.
- Don't have to be smart.
- Be genuine.
- The definition of learning is remembering what you are interested in.
- There's no such thing as a teacher—only a guide.
- Celebrate connections with others.

people interaction. Be such a person! Sandler Sales Institute conducted a study on the impact of a personal introduction on the sales cycle. They determined that

- Only 1 to 5 percent of cold calls lead to a successful sale.
- About 15 percent of referrals are successful when a name is given out. (I haven't worked with Susan before, but I know that her business helps start-ups create web sites.)
- The success rate leaps to 50 percent when a phone call or email is sent on your behalf.
- It catapults to the high 70s and over 80 percent when the person who can make the introduction attends the meeting or phone call.

These results are shown in Figure 2-2.

I called Jack to get his advice on a business idea. We had worked together a few times, and I can always trust him to tell it to me straight. "I'm not the person who can help you, Matt is. Let's get him on the line." The next thing I knew, I was part of a three-way conversation. I had never even met Matt. Jack explained why Matt would benefit from the business idea. At first Matt wasn't convinced and was dismissive. Jack addressed his concerns, and at the end Matt was on board and I had talked the least.

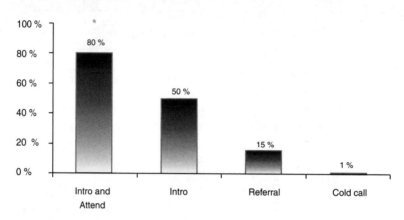

Figure 2-2   Value of Networking versus Cold Calls Chart

Summary: The more people savvy you are, the better your chances of success. The more you let others help you, the greater your success.

3

Getting Started

Conditions are never just right. People who delay action until all factors are favorable are the kind who do nothing. ~ WILLIAM FEATHER

Most people network when they need something—a job, a business lead, an employee, or a contribution to an organization. If you are networking now, keep going. If you are not, start immediately. In order to receive, you must give. The more you have given to others, the easier and faster it will be when you have a genuine need from someone in your network.

Networking is cyclical, and you can start it at any time. We are often hard on ourselves, assuming that we cannot help someone else. The more we give, the more we realize how easy it is to do so. It's often the little things we do for someone else that teach us the value of our knowledge. It's also important to learn how to ask for help. Later in the book, you'll learn specific ways to ask for help.

Many will tell you to make a list of your friends, work colleagues, family, or other contacts and start calling people. But you're going to do something else first—talk to complete strangers.

This may seem counterintuitive. However, can you remember a time when you were on a plane and by the end of the flight you knew the life story of the person sitting next to you? You were safe to talk to. The person didn't know you and therefore felt that he or she could talk to you about anything.

Put this book down and go for a walk or an errand. Smile and make eye contact with at least two people you don't know. People with dogs are typically very friendly. If you see someone with a dog, smile, walk up to them, and ask the name of the pet. Start the conversation by asking if you can pet the dog. Next ask what is the breed and how long the person has had a dog. After a few minutes, say thank you and then walk away. If you feel at all awkward, see the sidebar.

Next, go to the grocery store and shop for some food. While you are selecting a brand, ask someone in the aisle if she or he is familiar with the product or if there is another that she or he prefers. Again thank the person and walk away.

The purpose of these two exercises is to get you to talk to someone you've never spoken to before and ask a few questions. You are not asking this person to become a client, asking her or him to fund your business, or get you a job. That's a sales call, investment presentation, or a job interview. You are asking about a dog and about some groceries. You are also asking about the person or asking his or her opinion—both things that people can easily comment on.

Now, go do it. This will take only 10 to 15 minutes for each exercise.

How did it go?

Ask yourself a few questions and note your answers.

- What did you like about the exercises?
- After the first few questions, what happened to the conversation?
- Did you find out something more about these people?
- What area of town do they live in?
- What do they do for a living?

Things We Can Learn from a Dog

1. Never pass up the opportunity to go for a joy ride.
2. Allow the experience of fresh air and the wind in your face to be pure ecstasy.
3. When loved ones come home, always run and greet them.
4. When it's in your best interest, practice obedience.
5. Let others know when they have invaded your territory.
6. Take naps and stretch before rising.
7. Run, romp, and play daily.
8. Eat with gusto and enthusiasm.
9. Be loyal.
10. Never pretend to be something you're not.
11. If what you want is buried, dig until you find it.
12. When someone is having a bad day, be silent, sit close by, and nuzzle him or her gently.
13. Thrive on attention.
14. Avoid biting when a simple growl will do.
15. On hot days, drink lots of water and sit under a shady tree.
16. When you're happy, dance around and wag your entire body.
17. Delight in the simple joy of a long walk.
18. No matter how often you are scolded, don't buy the guilt thing and pout—run right back and make friends.

- How did you feel when the exercise was over and you picked up the book again?
- Did you wish you could talk to strangers all day?
- What didn't you like?
- How did it feel walking up to a total stranger?
- What would you do differently?

You have just accomplished one of the key steps in networking: communicating with a stranger and making a connection. That is where networking begins, and the more you do it, the more confidence you'll gain. As with any kind of exercise, you need to develop those muscles, and the muscle memory will help you to do it more easily and better the next time.

As you gain confidence in your networking ability, do the same exercise, but with acquaintances—for example, people that you see on occasion, perhaps a former colleague or someone you would just like to get to know better in business.

It can be quite intimidating to ask for help from people we are close to. We assume they know what we do and what we need. However, we can also miss an easy solution by not letting friends and family know what we are doing and how they can help us be successful.

> *Summary: Taking calculated risks has rewards. Try something new! Test your networking skills on strangers. It is easier, since it's likely that you will be less nervous and the risks are indeed much lower.*

CREATE A PLAN

> *Poor planning on your part does not create an emergency on my part.* ~ UNKNOWN

Pick a project you want to accomplish for which networking can be obviously useful. Maybe it's getting a new client or a new job. If you are involved with a nonprofit, perhaps you want to secure a grant or find more volunteers. Or maybe you have recently moved, and you want to take up a new sport—perhaps tennis or golf.

Throughout *The Networking Survival Guide* we'll discuss your goal and ways to achieve it. Perhaps on the path you will discover a nice detour. This happens all the time. We have a specific purpose in mind; however, as the journey continues, something wonderful surprises us, and we now have a new objective.

While it's important to have goals, don't make them so rigid that you can't switch gears if a better opportunity comes along or if it is just necessary to make a change. Lisa went to a conference.

Her goal was to get sales leads. It turned out that the attendees were not at her level. At first she was disappointed, but after hearing the first speaker, she felt inspired. She shifted her goal from sales to personal development rather than getting down on herself because she was spending time at a conference that wouldn't give her any new business.

No matter what you selected, your goals should be *smart*!

- S—specific
- M—measurable
- A—achievable
- R—realistic
- T—timed

What do I mean by networking goals? Here are some examples:

- *Business development.* Meet two people who can introduce me to decision makers who would want to purchase my product or service.
- *Raising capital.* Send an email to my network sharing the news that we are seeking a $1 million expansion round of capital and asking them to help identify the right investors.
- *Professional development.* Contact three people who have an MBA and ask their advice about whether I should get one as well.
- *Job search.* Set up one-on-one meetings with two previous supervisors who know my skills.
- *Recruiting.* Hold an internal networking session at the office to let employees know of new jobs or a referral bonus plan for new hires.
- *Nonprofit.* Identify five donors who would like to donate to the Brain Tumor Society.
- *Social.* Call three health clubs in the city to where I have moved and get information about their members to determine which one is right for me.

You have identified why you want to network and what results you are seeking. Now is the time to come down from the 10,000-foot level and get practical. In order for us to start on our networking journey, first we need to find the spot on the map that says, "You are here!"

Summary: When you plan, you save yourself time, energy, and money and ultimately you network smarter and less.

A FEW GOOD PEOPLE

Often I'm asked, "How many people do I need to know?" After all, networking could quickly become a full-time job and then some. One person can make quite a few introductions. Each person typically knows about 200 to 250 people. If you add just one person to your network each week, that would be 50 people in just a year. If each of them knows 200 other people, you automatically are two steps away from 10,000 people. Few can manage that kind of interaction and maintain quality networking.

Determine the type of people you want to add to your network. Then find the locations where those people hang out. Everyone can be useful in your life. Some are the decision makers, and others influence them. What's most important is that they share your values and their actions reflect the quality of your life.

Summary: You want quality contacts, not quantity.

INVENTORY YOUR NETWORKS

When I ask clients to inventory their networks, many say that they only have one network. Typically, that network is business-related. By the end of a few sessions, however, they realize that they have many more networks than they thought they had.

When your networks are identified and organized, it's easier to find the right person for the right problem. You can also start introducing people to each other. You are then viewed as a go-to person, and you become a networking "node."

Most of us have a toothbrush holder in the bathroom and a place where we put our forks, typically in the kitchen. It would be quite miserable if they got mixed up. This is what can happen when we mix our networks: We get a fork in our gums. Ouch!

When a company creates an organization chart, it simply identifies the roles that the firm needs in order to run effectively, and allows it to put the right people in the right job.

You are going to inventory your networks. This is a useful exercise that is fundamental to your networking plan. You will quickly realize that you know more people than you thought. As you do this exercise, note people's interests. For example, as you map your network, you'll recall that your good friend from college is an avid sailor. You'll realize that one of your work colleagues and also one of your neighbors have sailboats. This will give you a perfect excuse to introduce people to each other. You can send an email to each person introducing them, saying what they have in common, and telling them how each person can meet the other.

Why make the effort? This is an excellent way to increase your visibility in your community. You will become known as a go-to person. When people have a problem that they need solved, they will come to you. This extends your value.

This is an investment in your community and your business success.

Figure 3-1 is an example of what a network looks like. In order to do the inventory exercise, you need

- A piece of paper—consider getting something a bit larger, like a poster size
- A pen or pencil
- Post-it notes—different sizes or colors are helpful (or an eraser)

Personal Networking—"Who's the Ball?"

Ric Fulop, entrepreneur

"Networking," he said, "is like watching kids playing soccer. They all rush to chase and surround the ball. With networking, who's the ball? You want to be the ball."

Ric's family went from Israel to Venezuela, and he came to the United States for adventure. He is warm and charming. We discussed what benefit he may have given. English isn't his first language. He said he is able to ask questions if he doesn't understand a word or concept that might intimidate someone else. He said that approximately a third of the CEOs in Silicon Valley are foreigners. "They have the risk profile to run companies, they have beat the odds just getting here."

He is on his sixth or seventh company and clearly is having a great time. He introduced himself to someone as we left the restaurant, even though they had never met. Some of his insights on network success include the following:

- Establish credibility very quickly.
- Have a mental picture of whom you know in common.
- Be humble, not arrogant.
- Always have business cards.
- When shaking hands, be sure to look someone straight in the eye—it builds trust.
- Be approachable.
- Organize your business cards and keep them that way.
- Be ambitious.
- Be the best ambassador for your company.
- Have fun!

Let's begin:

1. In the middle of the paper, write your name in the cloud. (See the example in Figure 3-1.)

   Now you know the truth: You are the center of the universe!

2. Next determine what networks you have. For example:

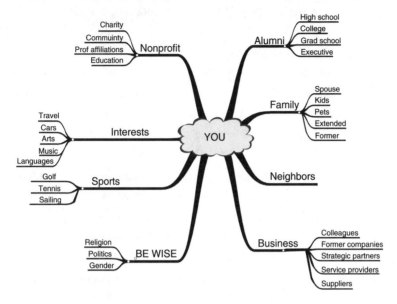

Figure 3-1   Map Your Network

- *Alumni.* List all the schools you have affiliations with and where you've stayed in touch with people. What are they up to now? Think of people who can be a resource for you and vice versa.
- *Neighbors.* This is often an overlooked category. Often we know little about those who live near us yet obviously there is a lot in common or you wouldn't have selected the neighborhood to begin with.
- *Family.* Kids and pets are a hidden gem in this category. Through them we can meet all kinds of interesting people. One's extended family is also a terrific resource. There can be a more friendly relationship in many cases.
- *Business.* This is the core network we will review. Don't forget about your previous companies. Corporate alumni groups are strong and loyal. This is an excellent resource for you to connect with.

- *Nonprofit*. There are many wonderful people you will meet who participate in a variety of nonprofits. They attract a cross section of people who share a common interest but come from a diversity of industries.

- *Interests*. Where to stop, there are so many! This is often where business relationships begin. People start talking and realize they share a common interest. Even if you don't participate, read about trends and what's going on.

- *Sports*. Most everyone has a sport that they either follow or participate in. For me, the day after the Super Bowl is a somber one—I just love football. The strategy, passion, and energy are enjoyable to me. I'm not particularly athletic so I try to learn tennis every so often.

- *BE WISE*. This is a collection of three areas that you want to inventory. However, you want to be very careful about overlapping them.

3. Pick one of the networks, let's say business. (If you want, use Post-it notes the first time you work on this exercise until you get the hang of it.)

4. As you identify your network, organize it. This will be a living document—in other words, as your life changes, so will your networking inventory. Just like writing a business plan, the first time you do it will be the most work.

5. Start with one network—for example, former colleagues— and do a complete inventory.

    - Write the name of each person.

    - As you are doing this, think of each person's hobbies, profession, and so on.

    - What do you know about each person?

    - What does each person know about you?

    - Will each person return your call? If so, how quickly? If not, why not?

- Whom are you comfortable calling?
- Whom would you not call? Why?
6. Take a break.
  - Every so often, stop and take a look at the bigger picture of who is in your network.
  - Make a list of people to introduce to each other. Why would they like to meet? What are their common links?

You'll notice that there is one branch on the chart that reads, "be wise." These are the people in three specific networks: politics, religion, and gender. It is important to manage these relationships carefully. While you may guess that someone else who practices your faith has the same political opinions as you do, it is prudent to be wise.

While it is valuable to inventory these groups, be careful how much you "cross-network," if you will. Unless you know that two people share a cause, doing so is a quick way to lose friends or business. You may have strong feelings about a certain political issue, and if you aren't careful you can alienate both friends and business associates.

One time I was at a "woman" event at the Kennedy Library. The panel included four incredible women who were considered trailblazers in their respective fields. At the time, the governor of Massachusetts was a woman who had recently had twins while she was in office. Opinions ran the gamut on whether she was a trailblazer or whether she confirmed the suspicion some had that women shouldn't hold public office.

I stood up to ask the women panelists what they thought of her and how she was being treated. The silence in the room was truly deafening, then there were a few hushed boos and hisses. I sat down and asked the person sitting next to me what was going on. "Diane, you asked a question about a Republican. We are at the Kennedy Library."

Summary: Inventory and organize your network. Take good care of it.

EVALUATE YOUR NETWORK

Now that you know who is in your network, it's time to evaluate each contact, his or her relationship to what you need, and, of course, how you can give back. Since each relationship is unique, so will your assessment be.

For each person, ask yourself how accessible he or she is and whether your call will be returned promptly (within 48 hours). Networking is more than whom you know. It's who knows you! The delicate difference becomes much more evident when you don't get a return call.

Networking gives you ways to stay in touch and helps you discover who those people are in your life. This is not a popularity contest like high school. This is not *just* about people we like; it's more than that. It's about people we can get help from when we need it and vice versa.

There are some basic criteria to use for everyone:

- How does he or she make me feel?
  - Am I energized or drained after being with him or her?
  - Do I feel valued?
  - Does he or she treat me with respect?
  - Am I heard?
  - Do I laugh when I'm with the person?
  - Do I have fun?
  - Am I given worthwhile feedback, or do I feel criticized?
  - What is his or her temper like? I find it exhausting when I'm on edge wondering if or when someone will be angry or moody.
- Is his or her knowledge relevant to my present needs?
  - Does this person have expertise that I need right now?
  - Will he or she be willing and able to make time for me?
  - Does he or she have access to others who can be of assistance?

- What can I give back?
  - Is there someone I can introduce him or her to?
  - Is there an organization or event that I can tell him or her about?
  - What compensation would this person like? For some it is cash; in other cases it's another currency—introductions, advice, referrals, time, or something else. Get his or her input.

Either people make you feel good or they don't. It's just that simple. This doesn't mean that you will always be told it's going to be a sunny beautiful day and everything is rosy. In fact, we often feel the most cared for when people are willing to give us heartfelt, genuine feedback. We are treated with respect and both parties are valued.

Do you have the right relationships in place for the achievement you are seeking? Here are some questions worth reviewing:

- Who has the power to help you (power as in access)?
- What do you need from these people? Have you written it down?
- What is the best way to approach them? Who can make an introduction on your behalf?
- What is your value? What problem do you solve?
- What is their value? What do they offer you?

Company or Organization

Evaluate the companies or organizations you have affiliations with. The goal is to give you a bird's-eye view of the relationship. This includes metrics such as

- Have you earned new clients from your association with this organization?
- Who was instrumental in making that happen?

- If the company or organization is a key client, what would happen if your contact left? Do you have other relationships in place?
- Has someone in the organization introduced you to someone you hired?
- Did someone in the organization introduce you to a new supplier?

For organizations where you volunteer, ask the same questions. In addition, what is your role with the group? Write it out. What is the value you offer and get?

- What have you accomplished for the organization?
- How much time do you contribute?
- When you look on your calendar and see that you have a meeting with the group, does that make you feel energized or drained?
- How long have you been involved with the group?
- Is there a natural successor to you? If not, why not? Consider finding one and mentoring her or him—this will get you visibility.
- How did you get involved in the beginning?
- Has the relationship served its purpose, or is there still more you can accomplish?

Figure 3-2 shows the company—we will do the people next. Create a profile for each company.

People

As you already know, you do business with people, not companies or organizations. Now we want to drill down and evaluate the people in each company or organization.

On each Post-it note, write three things:

Corporate Profile

Company	$ spent with them
Address	services provided
City, State, Zip	
Main Phone	
Web	
Industry	
Contact Name	CEO Name
Title	Last time spoke
Last time met F2F	Last time we met F2F
Introduced by?	
Met where?	
Referred biz to us?	
Outcome?	
Sent thank you?	
Referred employee?	

Figure 3-2 Corporate Profile

1. CB—this means the person will call you back within a week.
2. What you can offer the person (underline it).
3. What you want from the person (put it in quotes).

To start, create a business profile for the top and bottom 5 percent of your clients based on revenue or profitability. Get to know them a bit better. Review these questions and see what you know off the top of your head.

- Who are their service providers?
- When was the last time you met with them and didn't ask for anything?
- What significant milestones have they met or are likely to meet soon?

- Did you send a congratulations gift or take them to dinner?
- Have they made a hire recently whom you haven't met?

Make a list of the companies that are in the bottom 5 percent *and* have people whom you genuinely like doing business with. These people will help you practice new networking skills. To start out, ask yourself,

- Why do you like them?
- What can you do to make them more successful?
- Whom can you introduce them to?

Make this an excellent learning opportunity for networking. Much of what you will learn is how much you can give to others and how much they would be delighted to help you. You just have to ask!

Do the same with your top 5 percent. Don't make calls right away, though.

NETWORKING WITH PRESENT CLIENTS

Now that you've successfully inventoried and prioritized your present clients, you know what works for your business and what doesn't. After a few networking sessions, you also have a good idea of what patterns you see in your clients, what their needs are, and how you can help. In addition, you are learning ways in which they can help you. The more information you have, the easier it is for you to ask for their support. In order to maximize your time and effort, here is a strategy to use as a template.

1. Prepare. Put together a three- to four-point bullet outline about the person you are contacting and what you want from him or her. For example,
   a. Calling Jack Jones.
   b. Want introduction to Ms. Smith @ Smith & Associates.
   c. Would like to provide legal services.

d. We have expertise in mergers and acquisitions and can help her grow the company.

2. Call and ask for a meeting.

3. Let the person know that you are growing your business and would like her or his advice.

4. Set the meeting according to what's best for the other person—location, time, etc.

5. Pick up the tab for any expenses.

6. At the meeting:

    a. Be very specific. If you want an introduction to the vice president of marketing at a certain company, know that person's name and why you want to meet her or him.

    b. Create an atmosphere in which they can say no. Make it comfortable for the person to say that the timing isn't right or the relationship isn't such that he or she can do what you ask.

    c. WII-FM—what's in it for this person? Why should he or she help you? Is there a compelling reason?

7. After the meeting:

    a. Send a thank-you note within 24 to 48 hours—email or paper, whichever is more appropriate.

    b. Keep the person updated on your progress.

    c. Ask what you can do for him or her.

8. Repeat with each client.

NET VERSUS GROSS

I'm not sure how I would define *grossworking* even if I had to! Fortunately, as with our income, the net is what we really care about. It is what we get to keep. We refer to our safety net as a source of protection, a resource for us.

From lemonade stand proprietors to *Fortune* 100 CEOs, the difference between net and gross on a balance sheet is where the truth is told. Few people realize that the same principle applies to a network. When you take a look at all the people in your Rolodex (the gross) and subtract the people with whom you have the fewest reciprocal relationships, you arrive at the net. In other words, you want to focus on those with whom you have the most in common. These are the people you can help the most and vice versa. This is your true "net" network.

Sales professionals call this the 80/20 rule: You get 80 percent of your business from 20 percent of your clients.

A question that often comes up is how to purge names. I'm actually a believer in reorganizing rather than eliminating. I worked in the travel industry for a number of years, and I met a wide variety of fun and wonderful people. Now, however, we are no longer colleagues. As I reinventory the network, they move to a new group—vendors, friends, acquaintances, or some other category.

As you complete the inventory exercise, you have a visual reminder that networks are fluid and ever-changing. Whenever I look at my database, I am always thinking, who would like to meet whom? This is also an opportunity to reconnect with someone without stalking him or her. (See Chapter 11 on the difference between persistence and stalking.)

> *Summary: Who are the core members of your network, and what do you offer them? What do they offer you?*

HOW TO PRIORITIZE WITH WHOM YOU NETWORK AND WHY

Now that we have identified and evaluated the network, let's prioritize it and focus on the "net." We want to learn more about these people—what we have to offer each other, and why. People drive companies and organizations. They move from one to another, and ultimately all our relationships are with the person, not the company.

Now we need to do another exercise that is similar to the others, but focused on the individuals, not the firm (see Figure 3-3).

- Whom do you like?
- Who gives you business?
- Whom do you give business to, and why?
- Who makes introductions on your behalf?

Personal Profile

Business		Personal	
Name		Phone	
Title		Email	
Name of company		Spouse/S.O.	
Business address		Children	
City, State, zip		Spouse job	
Phone		Spouse college	
Email		Graduate school	
Web		Kids school	
What their job is		Kids sports	
Latest promotion		Kids awards	
Sent congratulations		Community involvement	
College		Spouse referred biz	
Grad school		Family pet	
Associations		Name	
Charities		Breed	
Board			
Hobbies			
Sports			
Awards			
Referred any biz			
Things to know:			
Allergies/Injuries			
Family situation			
Custom/culture			

Phone: 888-907-0900
Email: Info@EffectiveNetworking.com   ©2003 Effective Networking, Inc.

Figure 3-3 Personal Profile

- Who returns your calls?
- Who is fun?
- Who makes you feel good?
- Who makes you feel stupid?
- Who is on the executive team?
- Where did each person go to college or graduate school?
- What community organizations is each person involved with? What professional associations? What nonprofit boards?
- Where do each person's children go to school?

Now it's time to put this into action. Go to the list of clients you like. That's right, people you just like, whether or not they are key customers from a revenue perspective. The two of you have worked together for a while and built a rapport, as well as a trust. Ask each of these people to meet you for breakfast or lunch (find out what is best for the particular person). I would encourage you to stay away from your top 5 percent. Select from the bottom 5 to 30 percent of your list. The goal is to practice networking, and you don't want to be practicing on your top clients. The more you do this, the better and more comfortable you will be. Don't risk nerves in your first few meetings.

Tell your client about this project and why you are doing it. What would you like from her or him? Why did this person's name pop into your mind—do you want business leads or a job? Enlist his or her support. Explain that you want to take your career, business, or organization to the next level, and you realize the importance of widening your professional community. Ask his or her advice. Following each meeting, determine your next steps.

- Is this someone you should meet with on a regular basis— once a week, month, quarter, or year?
- What can you do to help this person?
- What did you learn from the meeting?
- Would you do anything differently? If so, what and why?

People grow and change throughout their life. It is worthwhile reviewing your networks periodically to see whether you have people in the right place for mutual success. For example, there may be someone you worked with many years ago. You were in different departments, but you commuted together. Now you learn that your firm is seeking a new head of product development. That individual was in your colleague network, then shifted to acquaintance, and now is a potential work colleague again.

It is easy to overlook the people in your present network. You can quickly exhaust yourself meeting new people when your present clients may have the answers to your questions and just need to be asked. In addition, you may determine that the relationship needs to shift into a new network. Or you may decide that your time is better invested in other things and it's time for someone else to take over this relationship.

Summary: By continually prioritizing your network you will discover what is the best use of your time—for you and for your business—and who are the people who can help you succeed.

WHAT'S THE STATUS OF YOUR "NETBANK"?

If you want to connect with someone, but are hesitant to do so, maybe you should take a look at your "netbank" with that person. We have a netbank with everyone we know. This is just like a regular account at a bank. Either there is a balance or it's empty. The quickest way to find out if you have a balance in your netbank with someone is to try to make a withdrawal.

- When you need to call this person, do you feel free to do so?
- Will it be awkward for you to call? If so, why?
- Has it been a long time since you last spoke to the individual?
- When this person last called you, did you take the call— whether or not you could help him or her?

"You Cannot Innovate If You Always Hang Out with the Same People"

Desh Deshpande, entrepreneur, founder of Sycamore Networks

I had the good fortune of meeting Desh when we were both on a panel for TIE Atlantic. TIE stands for The Indus Entrepreneur, and this is one of the most organized and effective networks I have ever seen. There were over 200 energetic Indian entrepreneurs—and me!

Desh is widely considered one of the leading minds in computer networking. At the same time, he is someone who can walk into a room, walk up to people, and make them feel important. He is revered for his talents and appreciated for his understated style.

During the panel discussion, one person stood up and asked what was the best way to network with Desh and get his attention. The following are some of his comments that evening and from our conversation:

- Start with a reason to connect with someone.
- Have someone introduce you.
- Know what you want from the person. Many people assume that he can help them when he really can't.
- Be sure to do your research before you approach someone.
- It's frustrating when people approach you, but they don't know what they want.
- Learn by watching others.
- Enjoy the mystery and getting to know others.
- Networking is ongoing—it never stops.
- Be focused.
- Be creative.
- Be sincere.
- Be helpful to others.
- You need people to get things done!

We have netbanks with people we have helped in the past. We may have made an introduction on their behalf, given them a job reference, made a contribution to their favorite charity, or introduced them to a tennis partner in their neighborhood, for example.

If you hesitate to pick up the phone, your netbank with that person is either nonexistent or too low. Here's how to remedy the situation:

- Make a commitment *now* to finding a way to make a deposit in that person's netbank. Do this ASAP!
- Ask for nothing at this time. *Wait.*
- Simply find something you can do for the person.
- Identify people you do have a netbank with. Can they help you? Will they help you? Why or why not?
- Take a look at your networking inventory. What is the status of your netbanks for others?

Consider the following three examples:

1. There is a prospect you want to meet. Recently you learned that your former boss went to graduate school with this prospect. However, the last two times your former boss asked you to meet for coffee, you said you didn't have time.
2. You like to have a fresh cup of coffee first thing each morning from the specialty shop at the corner. Every so often the person sitting next to you comments that she should go out and get a cup of a coffee, but is just too busy. Yesterday you picked up two cups and gave one to your colleague.
3. You are considering a job change. Last time, you were placed by an executive search firm. However, you got so busy with the position that you never sent a thank-you note or updated the recruiter on your success. Now you are miserable, and you want to call the recruiter to get some help.

Which of these people have deposits in their netbank? You got it right, the second person. It may seem like a little thing (see the section in Chapter 4 on falling on your face). However, when you call your colleague from the airport and say, "Would you please get the confidential memo I left on the printer and put it in my desk drawer?" what do you think will happen?

Summary: Start making deposits now. They don't have to be huge or elaborate. A friendly smile or a five-minute phone call can go a long way.

Personal Networking—"Build a Bank of Favors"

Pat Sullivan, CEO of Interact Commerce

Internet Commerce makes ACT, one of the leading software programs businesses use to track clients. Much of our conversation was about getting involved in the community and building relationships with people in local associations such as Toastmasters, industry groups, and peer forums.

I asked how, given his busy schedule, he picks the people he makes time for. Here are his thoughts, comments, and questions.

- Do favors for other people.
- Appreciate people who get to the point.
- Stay in touch with people. (Use email, but use it wisely.)
- Have they helped me in the past?
- How did I first meet them?
- Do they come across as genuine?
- Name droppers are a turn-off.
- Do they have something I want?
- Use technology (such as ACT—and he loves his Treo) to help you manage people. You can remember only so much.
- Make time for face-to-face interaction.
- Networking must be mutually beneficial.
- Do not participate in bait and switch—"I'd like to get you involved in a charity" when you really want to sell office furniture.
- Know what you do well. "If you are an engineer, find someone who can speak business in order for me to make time for you."

UNCLUTTER YOUR NETWORK

For nearly 15 years I worked in the travel industry. I met some amazing people. Then I changed industries. I see those people on occasion, but now we connect as friends.

On an ongoing basis, check your inventory and be sure people are in the right network. There may be times when it makes sense to move someone from a business network category to a personal one, or from a personal to an acquaintance network. Sometimes business or personal relationships live out their need. This doesn't mean that you dislike this person; it just means that she or he belongs in a different place in your life.

How many relationships can you manage and do it well? While we want to keep our network fresh and inspired, we can quickly have too much going on. The next thing we find is that we have too many commitments to too many people and nothing is well managed.

People We Hear from Only When They Need Something

We all know the drill. The phone rings, and there is a very friendly voice on the other end wanting to know what we've been up to. We engage in the conversation waiting for the request to come, and it almost always does. There are indeed people whom we hear from only when they want something from us. Determine what your tolerance level for these people is and how much brain space you allow them to occupy rent-free.

Unhealthy People (or Forget about It!)

Throughout our lives, we will meet people whom we don't connect with or who are just not healthy and/or helpful. In some cases they can actually distract us. In some cases we continue to stay associated with them for a variety of reasons. Perhaps it's a challenge, or perhaps we think we need to for some reason.

These individuals are a bit more complex. They latch themselves onto us, and we permit them to do so. Like the folks we hear from only when they want something, these are individuals who add little to no value in our lives. In fact, sometimes they are downright destructive. They create conflict and gossip and are a distraction to you and those around you.

This is not a network to ignore. There's the saying, "Keep your friends close and your enemies closer." It's important to know who your detractors are. On occasion, it may be necessary to talk to them. Confronting people often avoids a confrontation. The word *confront* has a negative connotation. The antonym is to *avoid*. When we don't express our concerns about how someone is treating us, they may not know that what they are doing is hurting us. When we are avoiding the situation, often it gets bigger and bigger in our minds. That can lead to internal anger which, if unexpressed, turns into depression.

What we need to do is learn how to express ourselves in a positive and productive way. What sometimes goes wrong is that we let out our pent up frustration and it's like taking a finger out of the hole in a dike. The power and thrust of the works are so strong that they shock the other person and the relationship gets more damaged instead of repaired.

Find an interactive class in negotiations. Be sure you have a chance to participate actively. It's not enough to sit back and watch. It's one of the best things you'll ever do for yourself.

If you find yourself blowing up at people, then a class in anger management may be an option. The truth is everyone gets angry, and they should. It's how it is expressed that determines what happens next.

In some cases it's necessary for you to be the bigger person and just walk away. As when two people are playing catch, simply put down the ball and refuse to play. It isn't worth your time and energy.

Summary: Sometimes it's just best to think of yourself as Robert DeNiro and say, "Forget about it!"

Grandpa's Shoes

When I was a little girl, I remember my grandfather talking about his two pairs of shoes—a black pair and a brown pair. He could well afford others, but that was all he needed. I remember hearing him tell someone about how he took care of his shoes. Each night he would put powder in them to keep them fresh and put shoetrees in to maintain their shape.

When I walk into stores these days, I'm often overwhelmed by all the things I can buy and how much I could have in my life if I wanted to. It's easy to trick ourselves into believing we never have enough. We need more. When purchasing things isn't expensive, we tend to buy more. Almost everything comes in a disposable version. [Mind you, for some products (e.g., diapers) this is a monumental improvement.]

However, it can be easy to think that way about our networks. Instead of caring for and investing in a few good, strategic relationships in business, we kid ourselves into believing that we have a huge support network, when it really is just acquaintances.

Many people have a Rolodex or contact database that is full of names. The question is, now what? How many of them do you really know? How many of them do you really want to help? Which of them would help you if you called? If someone doesn't know much about you, what she or he can do for you, and what you can do for her or him, the relationship is limited.

Summary: Surround yourself with quality people—they are your networking halo. You are the company you keep. Realize that as you succeed, there will be some people who are not happy with your success. Let them go and fly with eagles who want you to soar.

4

Preparing for Networking

When you're prepared, you're more confident. When you have a strategy, you're more comfortable. ~ FRED COUPLES

Recently in a meeting I heard the saying, "Proper planning prevents poor performance." It's such a refreshing statement. When it's curtain time—your presentation, job interview, donation request, or investment presentation begins—you'll quickly get that feeling of either butterflies or calm confidence.

Next, let's look at some tactical ways to prepare and best practices to get your confidence anchored.

Spectacular achievement is always preceded by spectacular preparation. ~ ROBERT H. SCHULLER

YOUR SUPPORT NETWORKS

A client was heading off to an important industry conference with a work colleague. When they met at the event, he was startled. She was not dressed appropriately. Her clothes didn't quite match, and her attire was too casual. The situation was all the more awkward because she was senior to him. How do you tell someone that her clothes don't look right—especially your boss?

We have only a few seconds to make a first impression. Depending on your age, you may or may not remember the streaking craze on college campuses in the 1960s and 1970s. I was a budding teenage girl, and I thought this was just magnificent. I also remember a magazine that provided a guide for streakers. As I recall, the suggestions were as follows: "Wear a hat, ski goggles, and of course good running shoes. Last but not least, stand in front of a full-length mirror. After all, we want to keep America beautiful."

It's always been important for us to take care of our looks and image. Packaging is just as important for people as it is for products. What's important is to maximize what you have. I have seen what some would call very beautiful women look completely unappealing, with a slouched posture, sloppy clothes, and a scowl. Yes, Tiger Woods is a great golfer, but what a smile!

When Bill Gates made his appearance in Washington, D.C., his clothes were professional, and his style was quite different from what we had become accustomed to seeing. Even David Letterman and Jay Leno wear a suit when they work. Their guests wear anything and everything, but that's not okay for the host.

"First Impressions," read the headline of the *Boston Globe*. The article was about the first game to be played at the brand new Gillette Stadium. There was less concern about the football. "There are bigger fish to fry. The Patriots' brass will be watching—and crossing their fingers—to see . . . how bad the traffic tie-ups will be outside the stadium."[7] Of course the New England Patriots wanted to win their first game after their surprise victory at the Super Bowl, but it was also important to the event management crew that the people attending the game had a wonderful experience getting to and from the stadium.

A client begrudgingly hired an image consultant. She was deathly afraid of losing her personality and individuality in her clothes and style. Instead, it was a trip to freedom. She now had classic clothes that were appropriate for the audiences she worked with. Her clothes were not a daily distraction, not to mention a source of angst. Instead, she gained confidence and felt that she was more a part of the business community she served.

Your friends are not your fashion advisors, nor are they responsible for telling you to change anything else about your person. Take charge. Find people who are specialists, hire them, and keep yourself up-to-date.

Create a "kick-off" networking support group. What is great about this is that you will learn things that are practical from each of these people, everything is easy to do, and you can learn this material *fast*. I call this my MMB Team—these people "make me better" or collectively they are a "director of first impressions." This group builds your confidence.

Start from the outside and move in. Begin with your clothes, manners, image, fitness, and health. The people of this team are the keeper of your first impression. That's their job—let them do it. Get out of the way!

I've heard people say that fashion and even manners are "little things." It's more important that people get to "know me for who I am rather than judge me before they get to know me." In a perfect world, that is absolutely true. But we don't live in one, so we can either spend time fighting our culture or accept reality and invest in being our best, on the outside as well as on the inside.

What Falling on Your Face Can Teach You about Networking

If you are still not convinced, see how "little" things can keep you from falling flat on your face.

- Stand up.
- Lean forward as far as you possibly can without falling over. You may need to try this a few times.
- What is keeping you from actually falling on your face?

- Yes, balance plays a role. What else?
- Your toes!
- Now ask yourself, how big are your toes compared to the rest of your body?

Pretty little, huh? My point is that little things matter. This includes appropriate attire, a proper handshake, good manners, and saying thank you. During the late 1990s and up to the year 2000, it was assumed that these things were "old fashioned." Taking care of these "little" things means that you can let others focus on the big things.

It's the little things that often get you rejected. Say thank you to your toes. In honor of them. Here are ten people you should hire to help you make a winning first impression (see Figure 4-1).

1. *Wardrobe/image consultant.* This may be one person or perhaps more.

   a. *Wardrobe.* It's getting more and more difficult to know what to wear these days. What does business casual actually mean? Hire a specialist to go through your closet. Put together several outfits that are appropriate for various circumstances and various times of the year. This actually makes getting dressed for work much easier.

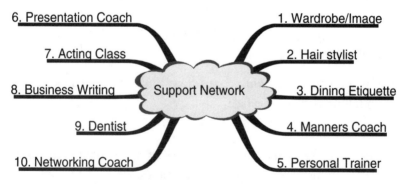

Figure 4-1   Support Network

b. *Image*. Glasses or contacts? Beard or no beard? Short hair or long? What color makeup? Find someone who can walk you through the choices and give you professional advice on your image beyond your clothes.

2. *Hair stylist*. Yale University did a study about the impact on our self-esteem if we have a "bad hair day." Gentlemen, it turns out you feel the same way. The three take-aways from the study were

    a. *Bad hair lowers self-esteem regarding performance.* "The perception of bad hair leads to a reduced sense of performance self-esteem. Just the thought of a bad hair day caused both men and women to feel they are not as smart as others. Surprisingly, the impact . . . was more pronounced among men."

    b. *Bad hair increases social insecurity.* "Women tend to feel more disgraced, embarrassed, ashamed or self-conscious. Men feel more nervous, less confident and are inclined to be unsociable."

    c. *Bad hair intensifies self-criticism.* "Evidence shows that bad hair causes one to be more negative about oneself."[8]

Find a stylist who listens. Find someone whose hair you like and ask where he or she gets it cut. Then forget about it—it's just one of your toes! How often do you think about them?

3. *Dining Etiquette*. Remember in the movie *Pretty Woman* when Julia Roberts' character asks the hotel general manager to teach her how to eat properly? Fine restaurants and hotels are teaching classes these days. Refresh your etiquette and meet some nice people in the process. Sign up!

4. *Manners coach.* For those of you who are fans of *West Wing*, you may have noticed that when the president walks in, everyone in the room stands up. It is proper etiquette to

stand up when a woman or someone more senior to you walks in. Opening a car door, walking on the outside of the street, saying please and thank you—manners speak volumes, just know them. Treating people with the utmost respect will only enhance the impression you make on others. For the ultimate in etiquette and manners information, go to the Emily Post web site, http://www.bartleby.com.

5. *Personal trainer.* Our body is the keeper of our mind and spirit. I made the decision to start a workout program last year. I hate to exercise. My rule has always been, I run only when I'm late for a plane. Within six months, my energy had changed, the way I carried myself had changed, and how well I slept had changed—my life was completely different. All positive. Find an exercise routine that works for you—just 15 minutes a day will make you feel great.

6. *Presentation coach.* Every time we walk in the door and speak to someone, we are indeed presenting. Hire an expert, not a friend. (Asking someone to critique you is a quick way to ruin a nice friendship.) Ask this person to coach you as you introduce yourself (see the section in Chapter 9 on introductions). Have him or her coach you when you give a presentation with slides or overheads. If you are hiring or interviewing, have someone role-play.

7. *Acting class.* Yes, that's acting like on stage. Find an adult education program that offers a short (four- to six-week) class. You already act now. You don't believe me? Have you ever talked to a baby? What happened to your voice, not to mention your words? Your voice pitch went up, and you forgot 99 percent of your vocabulary. Where did you learn to do that? Simple! You watched someone else talk to a baby, and when it was your turn, you "acted" the same way they did. When you are with your kids, you act one way, and when you are in the office, you act another. Push your

comfort zone. What's best is it's all for fun! Pay particular attention to your voice. If you spend time on the phone, consider taking a course in phone communication or radio announcing.

8. *Business writing.* Whether email or an annual report, business writing is an essential skill for the professional. Take a class that specifically teaches it—everything from style to content. For those who are well disciplined and can learn from a book, I suggest *Business Writing for Dummies*[9] by Sheryl Lindsell-Roberts.

9. *Dentist.* Only two-thirds of Americans have been to the dentist in the past 12 months according to the Centers for Disease Control. Your smile and oral hygiene are crucial. You do not want to be remembered for your bad breath. (*Note*: If you are ever offered a breath mint, take it. See the Resource Guide for where to buy a bad-breath tester.)

10. *Networking coach.* Last but certainly not least, find someone who can help you learn networking techniques and tactics. Like the others, this person needs to be trusted and have your permission to help you from the outside in. He or she is like a symphony conductor. On occasion he or she will probably work with others on your team to find the specialist you need.

That's a great start! Depending on your comfort level, you may want to visit some of these providers frequently or just every so often. Once you've learned what clothing styles suit you, a refresher every year or so is worthwhile. Practice business writing and attending networking events at least once a month. The more you do, the more you learn and the more confident you are. When you have a particularly important presentation to deliver, go back to your coach. Review this list every six months to make sure you have the support network in place to ensure a successful first impression.

Skills Training

Create your own personal graduate program as you advance in your career. To stay competitive you need skills now that you didn't need before. Many of these behaviors are ones that were not taught during your formal education—high school, college, or even graduate school. However, when these are mastered, they are the fast lane to success.

These providers take us a bit deeper inside. We have the wrapping paper all finished—we now need to add some deeper skills training.

1. *Management training.* It can be stressful to deal with a promotion, often manage people who used to be your peers, and balance new responsibilities. Sign up for a management course. If your firm offers one, take it. Also find something outside of the office so that you can ask questions you may not otherwise feel comfortable asking. Check with your human resources department for recommendations.

2. *Leadership.* Leadership training is vital for your career. There are essential, yet subtle differences between management and leadership. In some cases people can jump from one to the other. In many situations, however, people are naturally one or the other. Learn your strengths and then place yourself in a business situation where you can excel.

3. *Sales coach.* Yes, I know that for some people, especially for non-sales professionals such as attorneys, accountants, and doctors, to name just a few, sales is a nasty word. Job hunters are selling their skill sets, recruiters are selling their companies, executive directors of nonprofits are selling a mission. Each of us must "sell" every day. Networking can get you to the right person; however, it doesn't end there. The transaction needs to take place.

4. *Hiring and firing skills.* You are in the position to interview, hire, and on occasion terminate employees. Have someone teach you best practices. Be sure the class includes role

playing so that you can speak the words yourself, not just listen and watch someone else do it. A bad hire can be a drain on you and the entire company—financially and otherwise.

5. *Conflict resolution and stress management.* Potential conflict is a reality when you have two or more people in an organization. Even when we are all alone, we frequently argue with ourselves.

   a. Learn the subtle but important difference between confronting and confrontation.

   b. If we are able to confront skillfully without putting people on the defensive, we are likely to avoid a confrontation.

   c. Learn how to deal with differences in those you manage. Learn how different people are motivated. Realize where your buttons are, what happens when they get pushed, and how to deal with them. Understand the same about your employees.

6. *Meeting management.* As you grow in your career, you will run more meetings. Managing them well is a skill you can easily learn. Understand ways to construct the agenda, how to "park" a topic if the discussion gets off track, conflict resolution, timing, and ways to wrap the meeting up at the end so that everyone knows what's expected next.

7. *Time and project management.* You are the keeper of your schedule, even if others plan it. Discover ways to manage your day, determine priorities, and make time for what's most important to you, both personally and professionally. Our projects reflect our priorities as well as our organization and management skills. Study some techniques to help you process what you need to get done.

8. *Right brain/left brain.* If your job is finance, take a class in music or art. Develop an appreciation for the creative

process. If you are in the creative department, take a course in business management. Learn how to read and analyze financials.

9. *Communication.* Explore communication methods—what works well for you and how to communicate effectively with those with whom you interact. Include training in negotiation skills.

10. *Career coach.* Whether you are employed or not, it is worthwhile having someone you can specifically talk to about managing your career—how to come up with a plan of action for promotion, how to handle company politics, ways to gain visibility in your industry, or how to develop a solid résumé. Check in with your coach three or four times a year, not just when you have been laid off, have been fired, or are miserable at your job.

Personal Board of Advisors

In his book *Love the Work You're With,*[10] author Richard Whiteley discusses the concept of a personal board of advisors. Companies, universities, and nonprofits have a board of advisors, why not you? They provide wisdom, introductions, and resources to the groups they serve. Why not have a board that does the same for you? Put together a team of five or six individuals whom you like, know, and trust.

Whiteley's book identifies six key members of your board of advisors:

1. *Politician or mentor.* Mentor was a friend of Odysseus who was entrusted with the education of Odysseus' son Telemachus. Begin exploring a relationship with someone who genuinely wants to see you succeed and has the interest and time to mentor you.

2. *Strategist.* This person looks into the future to see what you will need and helps you create a map to get you there.

3. *Problem solver*. This person focuses on the present. He or she has experience with implementing techniques for getting past issues and moving on to the next step.

4. *Coach*. A championship team has one, so why not you? In fact, sports teams have defensive coaches, offensive coaches, special teams coaches. Depending on where you are in your life, identify what is holding you back. It may not be what you or others think.

5. *Butt kicker*. This person doesn't let you get away with anything. If you say you can't, your butt kicker will challenge you. Be prepared—this person will take you on an adventure.

6. *Cheerleader*. Whitely discusses the toxicity of negative criticism. One evening while I was hosting a networking party, a friend walked up to me and said, "You look tired." I wasn't sure what the value or purpose of that comment was, and I still don't know. Your cheerleader is not a Pollyanna, but she or he is a positive person who sees the glass as half full rather than half empty.

Discuss with your board what your expectations are. What is the time commitment you'd like from them? The more clearly defined this is, the better for all concerned. Consider putting the desired results on paper. Here are some examples:

- Within six months, we want to raise $1 million in venture money.
- By the end of the year, I want to be on track to make partner, and that means bringing in three clients with billings of $50,000 each.
- I want to find a new job in the biotech industry within the next four months.
- In the next six to nine months I'd like to be promoted to a position of greater authority at another company.

How long do you see this board being active? For example, if you are moving into a new industry, you may want to identify someone who also made a transition into that industry and ask him or her to be available for the first 90 days of your new job. If you are making the switch from for profit to nonprofit, find someone else who made the same decision.

Determine the "term limits" for your board members. This is important both for you and for them. Decide what should happen if the relationship just isn't meeting your needs or if they aren't comfortable with the role. What will you do? I'd caution you against holding meetings with your entire personal advisory board. I find that while these conversations can be inspiring and refreshing, at times they can be a bit draining. In most cases, you are seeking the members' individual, not collective, advice. Create a system that works for you.

Peer Group

Whether you are at the pinnacle of your career or just starting out, create a peer group. Do this outside of your company. For example, if you are head of marketing or engineering, find others who are in the same position. This group can be invaluable in your life. You can discuss topics that you wouldn't discuss with your management team, your board, your advisors, your investors, or your colleagues.

Here are some guidelines to consider for this forum:

- Rotate facilitators or have an outside one.
- Determine an agenda ahead of time and distribute it.
- Meet on a regular basis—maybe once or twice a month.
- Start with a six-month commitment from everyone.
- Define your expectations.
- Set confidentiality levels.
- Decide what constitutes a competitor.
- Determine how leads, referrals, and finder's fees will be handled.

- Write out a conflict resolution procedure and get agreement on the procedure. If this is difficult, it will tell you something!
- Determine requirements for participation and what to do if someone wishes to leave.
- Designate a time keeper and a note taker.
- Keep it to a manageable size—I suggest no larger than 12.

Networking Buddies

The first time I went scuba diving, I was terrified. I was loaded down with the weight of the world and plopped into the water, and I started sinking. What made the entire experience less threatening was my scuba buddy. A person I had never met before in my life shared an interest with me. Before we literally jumped overboard, he shared how nervous he had been on his first dive. As I somersaulted underwater, I righted myself to discover that the dive master was holding my hand. After a quick squeeze of the hand and a thumbs-up signal, I began to enjoy the warm, clear waters and a spectacular world I had yet to discover.

It can be frightening when you start to learn something new. Find a buddy, especially when you are attending networking forums. Some research says that walking into a room full of strangers precedes the fear of public speaking (which is typically listed as people's number one fear).

Have more than one buddy. You can have several for different situations. When reviewing your network for potential buddies, here are some things to consider:

- Select someone who serves the same customers but isn't a competitor. For example, you are an attorney, and your buddy works for an accounting firm that serves your same target client.
- Find someone who likes the same time frame you do—morning or evening.
- Is he or she someone that you trust completely?

A profile of your networking buddy is given in Figure 4-2.

The value of having a buddy depends on what you invest. This person is representing you in your shared professional circles. It is imperative that you spend time with each other so that you can intelligently answer questions and articulate what is wonderful about your buddy and vice versa. Here are some thoughts:

- Practice each other's introduction.
- Know about each other's achievements, especially recent ones.
- Determine your goals before the event.
- Agree who is responsible for the pre-event preparation (see "Whether Reports" later in this chapter),
- Review your buddy's snapshot (see the section at the end of this chapter).
- If possible, arrive together.
- At the check-in table, introduce yourself to at least one person and introduce your buddy.
- If you haven't eaten, have a bite together.
- Then, you *must* split up.
- One person walks clockwise and talks with people, the other works the room counterclockwise.
- Agree to meet at a specific time in a certain place *at* the event (for example, the bar at the far side of the room).
- Determine whether the event is worth staying for.
- If it makes sense to stay, loop back toward the front door.
- If not, call it a night and head home!

Qualities for Everyone in Your Support Network

You do not necessarily want clones of yourself. Little would get accomplished. For example, if you are a CEO, you want people around

Networking Buddy Profile

Name   _____

Title   _____

Company   _____

Direct   _____

Mobile   _____

Email   _____

Web   _____
     _____

Industry   _____

Professional association memberships

_____

_____

Years in business   _____

Board positions   _____

_____

What are networking goals?

_____

_____

_____

_____

Ability to meet at networking events?

         Morning

         Lunch

         After work

         Weekends

Hours per week buddy wants to network:

Time unavailable

Networking pet peeve(s)   _____

Phone: 888-907-0900   (c) 2003 Effective Networking, Inc.

Email: Info@EffectiveNetworking.com   p. 1/2

Figure 4-2   Networking Buddy Profile

My buddy's does:

_____

_____

_____

Their target industries are:

_____

_____

_____

Target clients:

_____

_____

_____

Present clients:

_____

_____

_____

Education:

_____

_____

_____

Professional associations:

_____

_____

_____

Board positions (past and present):

_____

_____

_____

Phone: 888-907-0900   (c) 2003 Effective Networking, Inc.
Email: Info@EffectiveNetworking.com   p. 2/2

Figure 4-2   Networking Buddy Profile *(continued)*

you who can make sure that the day-to-day operations of the business get done while you focus on long-term strategy. If everyone looked after the long-term plan, the business would suffer in the short term and potentially fail. Select people who have skills complementary to yours. If you are a vision person, find someone who loves looking at the present operation and how it affects the profitability of the business.

As you identify who belongs in your support network, here are some things to ask yourself. Some are more easily determined than others. If all else fails, trust your gut. Identify guidelines for acceptable and unacceptable behavior. Personally, I don't feel comfortable with people who have a temper. It intimidates me and makes me shut down. Typically, I arrive a few minutes before an event begins, which is frustrating for some people. If I know that promptness is an important attribute, I will be aware of my behavior and plan differently.

We all have our strengths and weaknesses.

- Does the person fit in with the others?
- Does he or she offer pertinent knowledge?
- Is there trust?
- Are you compatible?
- At the end of a session with her or him, do you feel energized or drained?

After you run through your list of criteria a few times, you will be able to determine if there is a mutually beneficial reason for you to move forward and begin to work together.

"WHETHER REPORTS"

These will help you to decide whether or not to attend an event, join an organization, or contact someone. Some of this will also depend on your attitude and latitude at the moment. You're going to create several "whether reports." For an event "whether report," see Figure 4-3.

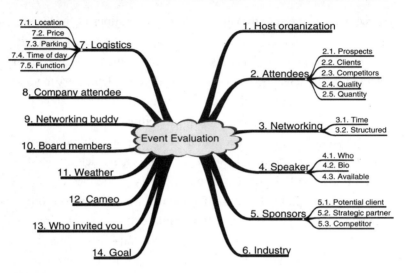

Figure 4-3   Event "Whether Report"

1. *Host organization.* Find out about the company, association, or organization and whether your missions and values are aligned.

   a. Who is the host organization?

   b. Have you attended this organization's events before?

   c. Do you know someone at the organization who can introduce you to others?

2. *Attendees.*

   a. Who will be attending and why are they there?

   b. If prospects, invite them to join you.

   c. If clients, be sure someone on your team greets them and makes a connection. If you do not, you can be sure that your competition will.

   d. Will your competitors be attending? Or are they perhaps sponsoring?

e. What level are the attendees? Do they make decisions about purchasing your product or service?

    f. How many will be at the event? In some cases, smaller events are much better. You have a greater opportunity to connect with the attendees.

3. *Networking.* In many cases, it's time with the other attendees that determines the value of the event. However, there is one event that I attend every year. I like to go because the speakers are excellent, even though there isn't any time for networking.

    a. How much time is allowed for networking? Is it before the event/speaker? After? Both? Be sure there is time to meet the attendees. You may be surprised, but this isn't always the case.

    b. How is the networking set up? Are there separate rooms for sponsors, vendors, or clients? Is the networking facilitated? At some meetings there is someone who keeps the introductions going and has an eye on the time.

4. *Speaker.* This individual often drives the event.

    a. Who is the speaker? Is he or she qualified to speak on the topic? Is this someone you would like to meet? If so, why?

    b. Check out the speaker's bio, which is typically available on the event web site.

    c. Will the speaker be available to meet with the audience after his or her presentation? In some cases, the answer is yes. In many cases, however, the speaker is swept away and you do not have any access to her or him.

5. *Sponsors.* Find out who the sponsors will be. This is another opportunity to make a connection or get some strategic information. Are any of them

a. Potential clients

    b. Strategic partners

    c. Competitors

6. *Industry.*

    a. Is the purpose of the event to enhance your industry?

    b. Is it to educate those employed in the market?

    c. Consider attending an event that is outside your industry.

7. *Logistics.* These factors can make or break your decision.

    a. *Location.* Is the event easy to get to from your office?

    b. *Price.* Is it worth the money? Expensive events can be worth every penny. Free events can be very expensive if you are trapped with an audience or speaker that is a mismatch for your goals. Consider other expenses: travel, lodging, clothing, and so on.

    c. *Parking.* Some cities are more conducive to transportation than others. Whatever your circumstances, know the costs and availability of parking.

    d. *Time of day.* Different opportunities exist at morning and evening events. Know the schedule and the goal of the gathering.

        i. For some, the morning is best. Others can't possibly leave the house early because of family responsibilities.

        ii. Know what you can and cannot do without risking your other obligations.

        iii. Remember, networking doesn't just take place at the office.

8. *Company attendees.*

    a. Who from your office will attend?

    b. Is he or she the best representative?

c. Is he or she comfortable explaining your product or service?

9. *Networking buddy.*

    a. If this is the first time you have attended an event with this organization, try to find a buddy to go with you.

    b. Determine which buddy is best.

    c. Practice each other's introductions prior to the event.

10. *Board members.*

    a. Do you know any of the board members of the organization?

    b. Are any of them prospects or clients?

    c. Email them ahead of time so that they know to look out for you.

11. *Weather.*

    a. This category can work for you either way.

    b. If it's a nice day, people will not want to be inside.

    c. However, if it's raining or snowing, they may not venture out of their office.

    d. Determine what works for you. Remember, safety is always first.

12. *Cameo. This is when you make a quick appearance, then leave.*

    a. If you must do this due to scheduling, let the host know in advance. If you cannot stay for the entire event, find someone from your company who can.

13. *Who invited you?*

    a. In many cases, this determines whether or not people attend an event. If the invitation was extended by someone of importance, they are more likely to attend.

14. *Goal.*

    a. Do you know why you are attending the event?

    b. What do you hope to accomplish?

c. When you leave, how will you judge whether it was a
     success or not?

An organization "whether report" helps you determine whether
or not to participate in the organization (see Figure 4-4). Just review
a few of these questions as you consider whether or not to participate
in an organization.

  1. Do you feel welcome when you arrive?
  2. Are the attendees in your industry?
  3. Are the attendees decision makers?
  4. What time of day are the events or meetings? Does that
     work with your schedule?
  5. Who is on the board?
  6. Is there an opportunity for you to add value to the organization?
     It can be frustrating if you don't have a chance to contribute.
  7. What is your goal for joining?

A contact "whether report" helps you determine whether or not
to contact someone (see Figure 4-5). It is worthwhile reviewing these

Figure 4-4   Organization "Whether Report"

"Business Card Is Your Passport"

Alan M. Webber, founding editor, *Fast Company*

Fast Company created a readers' network called Company of Friends. It has over 39,000 members around the world and hosts a variety of events in urban areas. The conversation with Webber started with his vision to "build a big tent and people will come." We then started talking about what people actually do at events such as Company of Friends. Here are his thoughts:

- Attend events that are out of character.
- Do something serendipitous.
- Notice something that you haven't seen before.
- Who invites him determines whether or not he attends an event.
- Business cards are your passport to the next part of the journey.
- Don't just hand out cards.
- Have a reason to meet someone.
- Find a way to bring value.
- Do something for them.
- Take notes.
- Storing and retrieving is hard to keep up with but very much worth it.
- Get beyond the formality.

Figure 4-5 Contact "Whether Report"

Personal Networking—"Win for All!"

Richard B. Colon, regional director of public affairs at Verizon and
president of the Latino Professional Association

I read about Rick in the *Boston Business Journal* and how his role at
the Latino Professionals Network benefits Verizon. The company realizes that Latinos are a fast-growing segment of the population, and
thus of its customer base. It is important for businesses to understand
their needs and to have employees that reflect their customer base.
Rick's participation in an organization that serves a segment of the
market that Verizon wants as customers is indeed a "win for all."
Indeed, Verizon nominated him for an excellence award for his contribution to his community.

I asked him to identify ways in which the organization helps the
Latino community and Verizon.

- The organization identifies high-value talent for recruiting.
- Latinos needed a network to create career opportunities and
  give them a community that connects them to mainstream
  business.
- The organization serves three purposes: career, education, and
  social.
- It helps people and companies identify success stories.
- As the Latino Professional Network gains visibility, so does
  Verizon.

---

questions before you make contact. In some cases, you may realize
that this person has already given you advice.

1. How do you know the person you are calling?
2. Who introduced you? What is that person up to?
3. When was the last time you spoke to the person? Did you
   take her or his advice then?
4. What are you asking for?
5. Have you written it down and practiced saying it out loud?
6. Are you prepared to hear no?
7. What about yes?

HOW TO QUALIFY A NETWORKING EVENT

Given the demands on our time, when we are away from the office or our family, networking needs to be worthwhile. It's hard to determine the value of an opportunity if we have not attended an event hosted by an organization before or if the organization is new to us. In addition to the "whether reports," ask yourself why you are going to the event. I recommend that you organize your reasons into three main categories:

1. Connecting with colleagues
2. Business opportunities
3. Personal growth

Connecting with Colleagues

An attorney at a bar association will logically meet many other lawyers. Attorneys have wills, real estate purchases, and other personal transactions that require legal review. It's less likely, however, that you will win a corporate account at a meeting of a professional association that serves your profession or industry.

It is more likely that you will meet others who will be professional resources for you. They may mentor you or vice versa. If you are considering taking an active role in the organization, this is where you can meet present committee members to learn more about the commitment. In addition, you can share stories of challenges and successes in your industry and gain good contacts for future career management.

Business Opportunities

At such an event you will see current clients and meet potential new ones. It is an ideal time to "press the flesh" and invest in some face-to-face networking. Clients like to see people with whom they do business in other settings. Make a point of introducing prospects to some of your happy clients. Find commonalities between the two—perhaps they have children at the same school, or they recently went on vacation to the same place, or they have common interests and hobbies.

Sporting events are natural for business connections. Companies have season tickets to take customers or prospects to a game. I was delighted to join four others one time to see the Boston Celtics play the Lakers. One of the reasons why golf is so popular with business professionals is that you can talk while playing.

Personal Growth

Professionals who want to grow their career are active learners. They attend classes, seminars, and conferences dedicated to enriching their knowledge of a subject. Typically there is time for networking at these sessions to meet both colleagues and business prospects.

Recently I decided to speak at an event because it was held at the new Ritz Carlton in Boston and I wanted to see the newly reno-vated hotel and meet the staff.

> *Summary: By taking the time to prequalify an event, you significantly increase the likelihood of a successful encounter.*

NETWORKING SNAPSHOT

The purpose of the snapshot is to give the other person some back-ground about you and also to share any special requests with her or him. This is a combination of a biography and a résumé, and includes personal data (see Figure 4-6). The snapshot provides conversation starters. After someone reads it, there are a number of things he or she knows about you and can ask. There may be some shared interests.

Smith and Jones
123 Main Street
Anytown, Anystate, USA
Phone: 321-123-1234
Web: www.Jones.com

Bill Bailey – Snapshot

Professional:
Partner at Smith and Jones. We help clients with all aspects of their legal needs.
My expertise is mergers and acquisitions.

Previously worked for state attorney, Tiger Tank Gas Company, and Best University.

Published:
Written several articles for legal journals including Lawyers Monthly.

Clients include:
Bank Three, British Express, Micronut, and Special Electric.

Residence:
Live in Anytown. Used to live in Memphis, London, Paris, and Cairo.

Family:
Married to high school sweetheart, Susan. Have two daughters, Sally (8) and Cindy (4).

Education:
Central University, South College and North High School.

Hobbies:
Sailing, skydiving, skiing, playing chess, watching football, and reading.
Former quarterback for Chicago Bears.

Associations:
President of the Any State Bar Association. Actively involved in the Anytown
Rotary Club. Coach daughter's soccer team.

Best way to contact: Bailey@Jones.com

Figure 4-6 Networking Snapshot

5

Networking Accessories

There are some basic networking tools that you should have at all times. Just like the scouts, be prepared! Depending on your destination, some items may vary.

BUSINESS CARDS

Cards are a part of life. In childhood you had baseball cards and playing cards, now you have credit cards and business cards. We feel grown up the first time we get "carded." No matter whom I ask, business cards are the number one networking must-have. Even people with sophisticated networking toys still carry and exchange business cards.

Just because you are carrying cash and credit cards doesn't mean that you are going to spend money. It does mean that you are ready in case there is something you want to buy. The same is true with business cards. Always carry them.

Given the importance of the business card, here are some guidelines from Janet Holian, vice president of product marketing at VistaPrint.com.

What Makes a Good Card

- *Design*. It should be clear and crisp, with good white space. It should say something about your business or yourself.
- *Font*. Use a minimum of 10 point. Pick a readable font.
- *Paper quality*. Use at least an 80-pound strength and 14-point thickness.
- *Job hunters*. It isn't necessary to put your home address on the card, particularly for women. Your phone number and email address are most important. (Consider getting a second phone line at home—your children or your babysitter wouldn't be answering your phone at work; why should they answer it when you are working to get a job? Or use a cell phone number if you are reachable on it in enough places and have voicemail.)
- *Home-based business*. Definitely have a separate phone line.
- *Folded cards*. These can be eye-catching; however, they are sometimes too gimmicky. They also don't fit in Rolodexes or go through card scanners. Use as a leave-behind card (discussed later in the chapter), rather than a business card.
- *Backside*. There are differing opinions here. Some feel that this should be left blank for notes; others say that this is prime real estate to explain what you do or your company does. If you do use the backside, consider leaving some space for the person to write a line or two.
- *Be sure all information is up-to-date and there are no typos.*

When to Hand Out a Card

- At meetings, cards are handed out at the beginning.
- At a networking event, cards are more typically given out after a conversation.
- Don't just walk up to people at events and hand out cards.

- Give a card when it is asked for.

- Ask for a card if you want to follow up. Mention that you will be calling; the person's body language will give you an indication of how he or she feels about this.

- Should you give out two? I've seen some people do this in the hope that you will forward it on. I don't carry around other people's cards, so I toss the second one away if I'm given it.

- If you are sharing someone's contact information (e.g., a referral), write it on the back of your card and add an arrow on the front—see Figure 5-1.

Sunshine Travel

John Jones
CEO
123 Main Street
Heartland, USA
212-555-1212
John@travel.com   →

Sally — call Kathy Smith at Smith, Snyder & Sinclair.
She can help you with your legal needs.

Figure 5-1   Sample Business Card with Referral

- Always carry business cards. (Yes, I know I've said it before —but it's important, so please don't forget it.)
- Be cautious about giving a card to a senior executive unless it is asked for.

Create a "Leave Behind Card"

When I give out my business card, I also give them a second card that has networking hints. The card often leads to a discussion about networking, people test their handshakes with me, and it creates a conversation.

I'd encourage you to do this. For example, if you are an accountant, have a card that provides some of the unknown tax deductions. If you represent a charity, write who you serve and what problem you solve. If you have a product, write out some of the benefits people experience when they use it. If you are recruiting a new hire, write out the job description.

This is very memorable and it gives people something that they can easily find later on. (See Figure 5-2.)

Card Cases

Your business cards reflect you and your company. If they are at the bottom of your briefcase, they seem like an afterthought. If they are stuffed into your pocket, it reveals the way you think: disorganized and haphazard. Respect your cards and put them in a case. They are your image when you are not around. Show others that you take care of them. Here are some ways to send a positive message.

- Carry two cases, one for your cards and the other for cards you receive.
- Inventory your case before and after each event.
- Resupply as needed.

Effective Networking, Inc.

Handshakes:
Two shakes, and let go!

Where to put your name badge:
On the right side of your chest (the eye naturally flows up the right arm as you are shaking hands).

How long to talk to one person:
Three to five minutes, eight minutes maximum.

Networking wardrobe:
When in doubt, go up a notch.

Take a networking kit:
A pen that you can lose, a Sharpie—to embolden your name on the name badge, breath mints, and business cards in a case.

What to talk about:
First, have a prepared tagline—what you're going to say after your name. Also come armed with three neutral questions, for example, are you from the area?

What not to talk about:
Personal stuff, sex, religion, and politics.

Eating:
Do not arrive hungry. It's difficult to juggle food with handshaking and business card exchanges. This is network, not net-eat.

Drinking:
Always keep your drink in your left hand. Otherwise your handshake will feel clammy.

Thank you notes:
How many handwritten notes do you get a day? Take an extra moment and write one. It's more noticeable than an email.

Figure 5-2 Leave Behind Card

Business Card Management

Finding someone's contact information when you want it, and quickly, is what matters. You can have the best and largest collection of cards in the world, but if you cannot find the one you need, it's just an exercise in frustration and you feel as if you are drowning in business card clutter. Find a system that works for you. Be patient, in all likelihood, it will change a few times.

There are several phases of business card management. They include

- Processing cards—what you do with them when you get them
- Storage and retrieval—how you keep them and how you find your contacts when you want to

Here are some tested ideas, suggestions, and products that I'm happy to share with you.

1. Processing.
   a. Start from the moment you receive the card. The process begins here.
   b. Your right-hand pocket is your cards (outbound); your left-hand pocket is for other people's cards (inbound).
   c. You shake hands with your right hand, so it's natural for you to give your card with your right hand.
   d. Look at the card when you receive it. Make a connection between the person and the card. Notice the color and design. Ask a question about the location—e.g., "I've always wanted to try the Italian restaurant on the corner. Is it good?"
   e. Have separate card cases. Then there will never be a chance that you will hand out someone else's card instead of your own.
   f. Immediately put the inbound cards in a container. Take them from the inbound card case and put them in an envelope or storage box. We all have experienced finding a business card tucked in a corner of our wallet or a very safe pocket in our briefcase, only to say, "Oh, that's where that card is." Depending on the number of cards you get, here are two ways to safeguard them.
      i. *Cassette box.* If I have been at a conference and have a stack of cards, I pop out the sprockets from a cassette storage box and put the cards there.
      ii. *Window or CD-ROM envelope.* Purchase a box of envelopes that have a plastic see-through window. You can get them at office supply stores. I particularly like the square ones that are used when software CDs are shipped. I take the cards from my

"inbound" business card case and put them in the envelope. The card that shows through the window is someone I particularly remember. Write on the envelope the name of the event, the date, and any other details. When the data from the card have been entered, I add a check mark in the top corner.

g. Screen and sort the cards:

i. When you return from a networking event, take a few minutes and review the cards while the names are fresh in your mind.

ii. Write on the back of each card what you promised the person you would do. Be sure to do what you said you would within five to seven days maximum. In some cases, note something memorable (discussed sailing, wearing bright pink, wants to travel to Thailand).

iii. A word of wisdom: Asians, particularly Japanese, take great pride in their business cards. It is inappropriate to write on a card in front of them.

iv. Sort cards by priority. I have one master database that I split off into two sections.

(1) Is this someone who wants to receive some information on the company right away?

(2) Is this someone who wants to be on your mailing list?

v. For my mailing list, I use Roving Software's Constant Contact to send out my email newsletters. All I upload is the first name and email address.

vi. If someone would like me to help his or her sales team learn networking techniques, that card is put in my active ACT database.

vii. Determine which cards you want to keep. The extent or relevance of your conversation will help you decide this. This becomes the "net" rather than the gross of whom you met. In this process, you are determining in which network they belong. Some people throw away cards. I still prefer to see the image of the card as a memory trigger. Some things to consider in general are:

(1) Did I like the person?

(2) Will I be able to add value to the person's business in the future?

(3) Will the person be able to help me?

(4) Does the person belong on my mailing list?

h. Convert the cards to a database for storage:

   i. Determine which software program works for you. Outlook and ACT are two of the more popular programs. If you need a true database that you can sort in many ways, I'd use ACT. If you need something simpler, use Outlook. Some people use a straightforward Excel spreadsheet.

  ii. If you prefer not to use a software program, see item 2 on storage options.

 iii. CardScan is wonderful. It scans business cards and then transfers them into a variety of software programs, including ACT and Outlook. It is quite accurate. It is especially useful when you return from a conference and have a large number of cards. It does not work for folded cards.

 iv. Data entry is your other choice. This is something I do while I'm watching a sitcom or some other TV show where my full attention is not required.

2. Storage and retrieval. Try different systems, ask others what they do, and be patient with yourself. No one I've met so far is genuinely satisfied with his or her method. Here are some techniques I use.

a. Categorize your contacts as you input your cards. This simple task will significantly help you later when you need to retrieve cards. If the time this takes seems frustrating, imagine yourself on the other end when you are seeking a card and you can't find it.

   i. Outlook calls them categories; ACT calls them groups. Either product can be used to create a system for inputting your cards. What is most important is to keep it current.

   ii. Sample categories or groups are mailing list, vendor, alumni friends, and colleagues. You can also use industry, such as financial services or technology. I use ACT to manage my names, and as I was working on the book, I created a group called NSG. This was a list of people who wanted to be notified when *The Networking Survival Guide* was available.

   iii. User fields can be customized, and I would encourage you to do so. Create two fields: one for where you met the person, and the second for who made the introduction. Sometimes both of these will be filled in; in other cases, just one will be. Then you can sort your database by either option. If you want, add a third field for the date you met. The help section of your program will provide instruction.

   iv. Business card sheets. What is good about this storage method is you can see each card. This is good because many of us remember people when we look at their card. Also, the sheets can be stored in three-ring binders. These can hold 10 business cards on each side. Because I write on the back of many cards, I don't use the back side of the sheet, so this method can get expensive quickly.

   v. Rolodex. This is one of the classic ways to keep cards. If it works for you, do it!

vi. Rubber bands. This is the storage system I most frequently find people using. It appears to be fast; however, it can quickly be deceiving. Trying to find a card can take a long time. If this works for you, use it. If this is the only place you have the data, be careful, since sometimes these stacks can get lost.

Summary: There are a number of ways to manage your cards—by last name, by company, by the event where you met, by type of vendor, or by some other category. You can use software, Rolodex, or even rubber bands. Use what works for you and your company.

PDA—TO BEAM OR NOT TO BEAM

With the plethora of technology toys, the question arises: Do we beam our business info or not?

The popular personal digital assistants (PDA) have the ability to swap information without the hassle of exchanging business cards. It's not trading the cards that's the hassle, of course, it's entering the data, filing the cards, and, most important, being able to retrieve the right card when we need to.

While researching this book, I discovered that few beam these days. Almost everyone prefers to get the physical card. They like it as a visual reminder and a tickler.

One time when I was beaming, I received not only the person's name and contact information, but also some passwords and credit card numbers. After I went shopping at Amazon, I called and let him know. (Just kidding!) Beamers beware!

I asked several entrepreneurs who specialize in creating products for PDAs, why not develop a "basket" to catch all the cards from a specific networking event? For example, ask the PDA to find all cards gathered from 7 to 10 A.M. on March 2, 2002. If you know of someone who can make this product, please contact us.

Summary: Have paper business cards and carry them at all times. Be careful when you beam.

NOTEPAD AND PEN

A few years ago, someone asked me to lunch and said he wanted some ideas on the travel business. I was happy to help. During the course of the conversation, I started giving him ideas and names of people who could help him. After a few minutes, I realized that he was not taking any notes—in fact, he didn't even *have* a piece of paper or a pen.

When someone is sharing information, be *prepared* to write notes. Ask permission first. It is unrealistic to expect that you will remember names, phone numbers, and emails not to mention the ideas this person is sharing. It's disrespectful to ask for his or her time and then not value the information that is shared.

The notebook or portfolio should be clean and simple. Get something classic and functional. Pull out a *clean* sheet of paper. The person would not be taking his or her time to share valuable information with you if you were not important to him or her. Treat the person with respect and send the signal that you value the information by using proper paper.

Always carry a pen. Personally I'd suggest one of three choices:

- Classic pen: Mont Blanc, Cross, Schaeffer, etc.
- Pen that's a conversation piece: antique, family pen, etc.
- Pen that you can lose (and that's not chewed—if you are hungry, get some food).

Make sure the pen works.

Would you go out of the house without your shoes and socks? Professionally, that's what you are doing when you are without pen and paper. Think back to the toes example—this may seem small, but it's an expression of you. You will fall flat on your face if you don't have the information you need. Like everything else, it either reinforces your personal brand or sends a conflicting message. If you act like you don't appreciate the information you are given, people won't take the time to help you.

BRIEFCASE

This is an extension of your image. Maximize the opportunity by owning a classy bag that complements your look. Personally, I like briefcases that are very easy to open, have some pockets, but not too many, and are well made. Levenger and Coach are my two favorite makers of briefcases.

Here are some things to keep in mind when you go briefcase shopping:

- How much weight do you want to carry? Some bags quickly get heavy.
- Classic or funky? Funky can get tiring fast. Functional is better.
- Leather or nylon? If you travel in areas where it frequently rains, consider a nylon bag.
- Entry. Can you open the case with one hand and keep your eye on the person with whom you are speaking?

Quote from Steve Leveen, president and cofounder of Levenger:

> *For the past couple years we've made it an informal mission to try to determine what the ideal briefcase would look and feel like. What we're finding is that the ideal is not one briefcase at all but in fact a wardrobe of briefcases for different people that fit different ways of working.*
>
> *I have a soft briefcase that's my weekday mainstay. But on weekends, I prefer a heavy-duty nylon bag that I can toss into my Jeep or boat along with my dog. When I'm interviewing people for my column on how successful people work, I want only my laptop and a few notes, so a*

*laptop case becomes part of this wardrobe. I think you'll
see laptop cases becoming more of a mainstay as more of
us carry our mobile office with us.*

*What's important is not just the looks and feel, but the
functionality of different briefcases. Few of us confine our
work to a traditional office setting anymore.*

CELL PHONES, PAGERS, AND OTHER THINGS THAT BEEP

Cell phones and other communication tools are a part of our lives.
Sometimes they are very useful devices that facilitate and streamline
communication. Other times they are a nuisance and can have a very
negative impact on those around you. Whenever there is a ring, you
have a choice. At that moment, your actions indicate your priorities
—who is more important, the person you are speaking with or the person calling. It's decision time. Your decision reflects on your personal
brand. It tells the other person who is more important.

We have all experienced the awkward feeling of finding ourselves
part of a conversation that we really don't want to be in the middle of,
such as arguments between work colleagues or business negotiations
that are less than pleasant. Not only is this unprofessional, but it can
also be detrimental to your success. A story was shared with me about
someone on a commuter train using a cell phone to complain about
someone he worked with. Another person from the firm was also on
the train, and the overheard conversation was reported to human
resources and quickly derailed the individual's career at that firm.

As with any other form of technology, it isn't the object itself
but how we use it that matters. Consider your surroundings and determine what's best. This means that you understand and respect the fact
that cell phone conversations are public and that the exchange may
not be one that should be broadcast.

If you cannot manage your technology, you are sending the signal that you may not be able to manage a project, or a new job, or to

use a contribution to a nonprofit wisely. This is a negative signal that can sabotage the likelihood the two of you will work together. Here are some pointers:

- If you are expecting a call that cannot be missed, tell the other person. This is less annoying to someone you are meeting with if you are upfront and honest about it. Let the person know the circumstances ahead of time, and apologize in advance that your meeting may be interrupted. Speak briefly and hang up right away, then turn off your phone.

- Ring volume can downright take your breath away! I've nearly jumped out of my skin when someone's phone went off. Invest a few minutes of time in getting to know your phone and where the buttons are—especially volume.

- Most phones come with a variety of clever rings. Find one that is distinctive to you, but not utterly annoying. Yes, the attention can be fun; however, it can also make you look quite unprofessional.

- Turn it to vibrate or silent.

Summary: If you are able to manage your technology, you are sending the message that you are able to manage other things in your life. That's a positive message to send and one that is appreciated by many.

6

Body Language, Voice, and Words

When we speak in person we use three communication methods: words, voice/tone, and body language. Professor Albert Mehrabian from UCLA[11] researched these carefully, and here is what he determined: We communicate 55 percent using our body language and 38 percent using our voice, tone, and pitch; our words account for only 7 percent of our communication power (see Figure 6-1).

Maybe this is where the phrase "actions speak louder than words" came from. Even plastic surgeons have noted the impact that body language can have on someone's career. When asked to identify good candidates for Botox, they list "executives, attorneys, and salesmen."[12]

In an article in the *San Francisco Chronicle*, the author noted, "Politicians, trial attorneys and others whose livelihoods depend on a deadpan expression will be able to realize great gains over their un-Botox-enhanced fellows."[13]

BODY LANGUAGE

Given what we now know about the power of body language, note the impact of body language on the "mood" of the image.

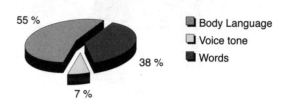

Figure 6-1 Body Language, Voice, and Words
Source: "Decoding Inconsistent Communication," Prof. Albert Mehrabian, UCLA.

Here are some guidelines:

- Have at least 18 inches of personal space around you when you talk to others.
- No slouching. Shoulders should not be confused with earrings.
- Shoulders and hips parallel.
- Smile!
- Maintain good eye contact without staring.
- Keep your hands out of your pockets.
- Gentlemen, don't rattle change in your pocket—this is very distracting!

These exercises illustrate how a few shifts in body language can significantly affect your experience with another person.

Exercise 1

- This requires two people and two chairs.
- Set the chairs up so that the people have their backs to each other.
- Each reads the following:

Susan: "Hello, I'm Susan Smith."
George: "Hi, Susan—I'm George Jones."
Susan: "Have you been to this meeting before?"
George: "I have. I really like the group. I take it this is your first visit."

Susan: "I attended a session a few months ago, and then I got busy. What do you do?"

George: "I help manage companies. Right now I'm with a pharmaceutical company, and we create drugs that reduce fever in children."

Now stop.

- What did talking with your backs to each other feel like?
- Did you feel that the other person was listening?
- Did you feel that he or she was interested in continuing the conversation or stopping as soon as possible?

Exercise 2

- Turn your chairs around, sit down, and face each other.
- Repeat the same dialogue.

Let's review:

- How did it feel?
- Was it different when you were facing each other?
- Discuss what felt different.

Exercise 3

- Now stand up and move the chairs out of the way.
- Stand a few feet apart as if you were at a cocktail party.
- Cross your arms and avoid eye contact.
- Repeat the same dialogue.

Please review:

- Describe how it felt.
- You become more engaged in the dialogue when you are standing.
- Also, you tend to pay closer attention when you are speaking.

Exercise 4

- Stay standing.
- Drop your arms to your sides.
- Reach out and shake hands.
- Look each other straight in the eye when you say your name.
- Repeat the dialogue.

As your body language shifts, so does your attention and commitment to the conversation. When you are speaking with someone, face toward him or her as much as feels comfortable. This may feel a bit intimidating in the beginning; however, the more you practice, the better it will feel. When your arms are across your body, this is an unfriendly signal—you are guarding your heart and chest area.

It takes practice and calm confidence to feel open and safe while engaging in a conversation with someone you don't know.

VOICE AND TONE

In the film *Three Men and a Baby*, there is a scene in which Tom Selleck's character is reading to the baby. His voice sounds like he is reading a children's story. When challenged by his roommates, he points out that it doesn't matter that he is reading the sports section of the newspaper; what is important is his tone of voice.

Question or Answer—Inflection

Listen to people talk. It's curious how many sound as if they are asking questions, when in fact they are making statements. It even happens when you first meet someone.

Do you make a statement or ask a question? "I'm Diane Darling?" Are you really sure? This isn't a question—this is a true statement.

Practice saying your name as a statement.

Do it again. Now a third time. Hear the difference?

Now add an additional sentence about what you do. For example, "Effective Networking helps organizations create a 'people' networking plan and helps people refine their networking skills."

Again, this is a statement. I've heard people say "I'm a VP of Marketing?" with their voice going up at the end. Are you sure you are? Why raise doubt? If you don't believe you are the VP, why should anyone else?

Now put it all together. "I'm Diane Darling from Effective Networking. We help organizations create 'people' networking plans and help people feel confident when they network."

Is Your Voice Smiling?

When you talk to someone on the phone, you can hear him or her smile. The voice has energy, enthusiasm, and a sense of purpose. The next time the phone rings, smile before you answer it. Consider standing up. That call is important. When we hear a content voice, we feel calm and assured that we are dealing with a friendly professional.

On the other hand, if the other person is speaking fast and seems agitated, the feeling is just the opposite. "Please don't bother me," this says. We've all heard the angry voice. Take the time to tape yourself. I don't know anyone who really likes her or his voice, however, it's what you have. Learn some techniques to help maximize your communication power.

It isn't certain where the word *phony* came from. The dictionary suggests that it came from a brass ringing sound in an Irish "confidence" game. Others say it came from the word *phone*. Does your tone of voice sound genuine or lacking in confidence? Do you come across as if you really are interested in the conversation you are having?

Take charge of the pace. If someone is anxious, slow your speech down. If the conversation is dragging, pick up the pace.

Don't mumble or talk too softly. Most people don't read lips and do want to hear what you have to say. Talk at a pitch and volume appropriate for your setting. Find a voice buddy at work who frequently hears you on the phone. Let him or her know that you are working on improving your voice skills and ask his or her assistance.

Summary: Given that we now know that our nonverbal skills are so important, take the time to stretch your skills and learn new techniques.

CHAPTER 6

WORDS

If you look at a brick building, you will see that the cement holding the building together is much smaller than the bricks; however, it keeps the structure from falling over. Your words are the same. When we talk with someone who doesn't speak our language, we immediately feel as if we have our hands tied behind our back.

While body language and tone of voice make up 93 percent of your communication power, you need quality, powerful, and carefully chosen "glue" to hold it all together. This is where your words come in. Here are some thoughts:

- Select a vocabulary level that is appropriate for the audience.
- Acronyms are great if everyone in the meeting knows what you mean. Otherwise, you sound like you are talking down to them. Also, the same acronym can mean different things to different people.
- Sports analogies work if your audience plays the sport. If not, you risk alienating your listeners.
- Refrain from slang or vulgarities or clichés.
- Speak in complete sentences.
- Use proper grammar.
- Get videotaped periodically and view the videotape (preferably with your presentation coach) for immediate feedback on all these topics.

Summary: For maximum networking success, be aware of all three aspects: body language, voice/tone, and your words. Consider this: When we send an email, we forfeit 93 percent of our communication power!

7

Conversations

When you have a taste for exceptional people, you always end up meeting them everywhere. ~ MAC ORLAN

At the heart and soul of any networking interaction is a conversation. When people share stories, interests, and ideas, they build rapport. When a connection is established, people want to continue to listen. In business, it is essential to get someone's attention first in order to continue and potentially do business together. How you are perceived in a discussion affects how you will be judged professionally.

Good conversation helps you win on two levels:

1. It strengthens self-confidence (a trait others want to see).
2. It makes you memorable.

CONVERSATION STARTERS

There are two types of people. Those who come into a room and say, "Well, here I am!" and those who come in and say, "Ah, there you are." ~ FREDERICK L. COLLINS

"Networking Creates a Placeholder for Future Contact"
~ TED DINTERSMITH, PARTNER, CHARLES RIVER VENTURES

I had been told by several people that Ted was a good conversationalist, and I was curious to learn if there were any particular techniques that he used. He seemed a bit bemused when I called, and he said he actually finds that many conversations fall into the same pattern—"I can't believe your kids have grown so much," for example.

As his profile has increased, he finds that there are two groups of people who approach him:

- Those who feel that they need to tell him everything in the next two to three minutes
- Those who know the "ground rules" (about 10 percent of those who approach him, in his mind)

When we spoke further about the ground rules, he talked about how people genuinely want to "create a placeholder for future contact." They know they cannot possibly explain everything about their business idea at a networking encounter. So they find someone they know mutually, either get introduced or introduce themselves at the event, and ask for a follow-up meeting.

His suggestions for conversations:

- Think through what you want to say.
- Talk about things you'd like to learn.
- Business conversations are more interesting when there is a personal story behind them.
- Too often people shy away from the personal story.
- Don't try to cram everything into one conversation.

Here are some ways to start conversations:

- Prior to the event, prepare three neutral questions you can ask, such as

  - Tell me how you know the host, company, etc.
  - What made you decide to come to this event?

- What other organizations in the _____ industry do you belong to?
- Focus on neutral topics. Here's a list:
  - Have you ever been to one of these events before?
  - Is the location near your home?
  - The latest news on the local sports team
  - Be observant—what is around you? A special attraction, park, etc.
  - What business you are in
  - Movies
  - Books
  - Sports you play
- Here are some ways to replenish your conversation starter repertoire:
  - Read the newspaper. Just skim the headlines and top stories. This can take as little as 15 minutes.
  - Watch national and local news.
  - Look at three types of magazine covers: news (*Time* or *Newsweek*), business (*BusinessWeek, Fortune*, or *Forbes*), and general interest (*People)*. Each cover is a conversation starter.
  - Know what's happening in the business world even if you don't work in it. This affects you directly or indirectly and is often a conversation starter.
  - Know how your home team is doing—the same is true with sports.
- Begin with a smile, eye contact, and an outstretched hand.
- This is the beginning—it doesn't need to cover every subject possible.
- Make it simple!
- Comment on a man's tie, or a woman's earrings, scarf, or pin. Stay with neutral comments to build rapport so you won't be

accused of flirting or sexual harassment—"I'd like to get something like that for my brother or sister."

- If you're feeling nervous, you're thinking too much about yourself. This is about making the *other* person feel important.

SMALL TALK

Effective questioning brings insight, which fuels curiosity, which cultivates wisdom. ~ CHIP BELL

Conversations typically start with small talk. Some people undervalue this exchange as mindless and an evil necessity. Think of the start of a dialogue as first gear in your car. While you may get going if you start in third or fourth gear, it isn't typically a pleasant way to start. You lurch forward and perhaps stall.

- Ask open-ended questions, then shut up and listen.
- Don't just talk about yourself.
- Participate in the discussion—don't wait for someone else to initiate.
- Don't answer questions with just one or two words.
- Lead the conversation to a new topic if the present one is getting inappropriate or not going anywhere.
- Compliment someone on his or her attire or a recent accomplishment.

SOME GUIDELINES FOR GOOD CONVERSATIONS

For some people, conversation comes easily. For others, it feels like a dreaded chore. Like anything else, this takes practice. Conversations are a part of life, and the more you try, the better you will become. Before too long, others will ask you to teach them. Here are some guidelines:

- Listen—you were given two ears and one mouth, take the hint!
- Don't be afraid to laugh, especially at yourself.
- Be aware of your body language and pay attention to the other person's.
- Be sincerely interested in others.
- Find commonalities.
- Remember that "thank you" and "please" are your two golden keys.
- Respect the other person's views.
- Remember that everyone's ego is fragile.
- Engage those around you.
- Don't interrupt.
- Don't finish other people's sentences.
- Don't control the conversation.
- Include others.

WHEN TO BREAK INTO A CONVERSATION

This is one of the more challenging and intimidating moments—when you walk in and there are conversations in progress. Others are participating, and you want to join, but how? Here are some thoughts:

- When there are just two people, I don't recommend breaking in.
- When there are three or more, it's fine.
- Catch the eye of one of the group members.
- Smile as you walk up.
- Offer your hand.
- Introduce yourself and explain how you fit into the event— e.g., "I'm Diane Darling, and this is my first visit to the Mickey Mouse Club. Minnie invited me."
- Ask a question, e.g., how long have each of you been members?

CONVERSATION TOPICS TO BE WARY OF

Here is a list of topics that *can* be delicate. This doesn't mean that you always need to steer away from them. But you need to approach them gently and cautiously. Be prepared to switch topics if the conversation gets contentious or if damage could be done to a relationship that is important to you.

For example, during an election, politics is headline news. There are choices in your conversation. Asking if someone watched the debates or encouraging someone to express his or her opinions by voting is one thing. Urging someone to believe a certain way about a topic such as abortion or the death penalty is tempting an argument.

What do you really want to accomplish? If your goal is to have someone think the way you do, that's fine. Engage in a conversation. If this is a business exchange, shift away from these topics:

- Politics
- Gender/sex
- Religion
- Weight
- Age
- Others at work
- Inappropriate jokes that could be offensive
- Getting too personal or sharing lots of personal information about yourself

HOW TO TRANSITION A CONVERSATION

The real art of conversation is not only to say the right thing in the right place, but to leave unsaid the wrong thing at the tempting moment. ~ DOROTHY NEVILL

On occasion we are in a conversation and realize that it is en route to becoming a runaway train. We sit there feeling a bit helpless as the conversation picks up speed and we begin to feel our uneasiness increasing. Think and think carefully! If the rapport between the two of you can withstand some friction, continue. If not, move the conversation to something more neutral and comfortable for you.

I was a dinner guest, and at one point the host asked a few questions about politics. I answered them politely and then realized that he wanted to debate rather than hear my point of view. The topic was a delicate one, and I could see that this was only going to get worse. At one point, I glanced over to the other side of the room and asked a question about the painting on the wall. I kept discussing the art in the home, and the discussion never returned to the delicate subject. When a conversation begins to go astray, take charge of your share. Decline to talk about anything you don't want to, and offer up a new topic.

HOW TO EXIT FROM A CONVERSATION

I've always been interested in people, but I've never liked them. ~ W. SOMERSET MAUGHAM

One of the questions I am asked most frequently is how to move away from someone without being rude. The conversation has reached its peak. There isn't much more to discuss. This happens on occasion when you meet someone who sells a product or service that you're not interested in. Do this person a favor and let her or him go talk to someone else. You are both nice people, but this is a business opportunity, and you both need to move onto other conversations.

Truthfully, the other person would probably like to move on as well, but he or she is just as nervous as you are. He or she has established a comfortable level with you. Starting a new conversation is work, so why bother. Why change a good thing?

Here are some pointers:

- Simply smile and say, "It was a pleasure meeting and/or talking to you, enjoy your morning, evening, or the presentation."

- Include someone nearby in your conversation. When the two of them begin to converse, excuse yourself and get involved in a new conversation.
- Invite the person to join you as you walk over to the bar or food table. Typically you will meet at least one or two people you can include in your conversation.
- Lying will make you feel dishonest because at that moment you are. Don't do it. Typical lies:
  - "I'm off to the restroom."
  - "I'm going to refresh my drink."
- Never leave someone alone.
- In some situations, the conversation is interesting and merits another meeting. This frequently happens in a social situation where it just isn't appropriate to continue talking business and where you're likely to get interrupted at some point. Take charge! Don't risk being interrupted. Say to the other person that you'd like to follow up, ask for his or her card, shake hands, and move on. (See the section on business cards in Chapter 5 for guidelines on when to hand them out.)
- When you are involved in an organization and you have a role, you also have permission to say to someone, "It's been nice talking to you. I need to say hello to others in the room, since I'm head of membership and that's my job here."

LISTENING SKILLS

Be a good listener. Your ears will never get you in trouble.
~ FRANK TYGER

Every moment people are talking, they are giving you an opportunity to offer help. Think about who in your network can help them. Make the introduction and make everyone happy.

When you listen, you can problem-solve for others. This doesn't mean that you need to do all the work. Just recommend someone in your network who can help.

Here are some recommendations to help you improve your listening skills:

- *Stand up.* This works very well for people who are distracted when talking on the phone.
- *Don't do anything else.* Imagine that the person is right in front of you and deserves your total attention.
- *Face the person.* When you are standing a bit at an angle, it sends the message that you want to be open to leaving the conversation and are less interested.
- *Make eye contact.* Be aware of connecting to the other person every so often. Look at the color of his or her eyes—it's a great way of making good eye contact.
- *Count to three before you speak.*
- *Most important, concentrate on the other person's agenda not yours.*

When you are focused on the other person, you come across as more confident. If your call really isn't genuine or you just want to make the connection to advance yourself, the other person can sense it quickly.

I was introduced to someone who was in charge of putting together events for an alumni association. We talked about dates for a presentation, what the group was looking for, who would be in the audience, and the typical questions I ask before a presentation. However, he quickly volunteered that he was unemployed and that this would be a good project for him to work on. He then shared with me the details about what he was looking for, how much networking he had done, and all the barriers that made it difficult for him to get a job.

He was a genuine person, and he certainly didn't realize that his actions were completely making me want to get off the phone and stay away! He talked too much and gave me too much information, and while he seemed eager to learn, his tactics indicated that he actually was not interested in improving his skills.

You may legitimately not know that you are doing something that is disruptive to someone else. I had a former boyfriend who used to finish my sentences. I finally said something about it. He then interrupted me and finished my sentence by asking what was my point.

We all have quirks. Find someone who is willing to tell you which of yours are charming and which are best unlearned. Talking too much can destroy a conversation very fast and is not uncommon. It usually happens when we are nervous. Be good to yourself and learn what are your strengths and what are your opportunities.

Summary: Knowing yourself can catapult you to networking success.

HOW LONG TO TALK TO SOMEONE

Some people can stay longer in an hour than others can in a week. ~ WILLIAM DEAN HOWELLS

We all want to be remembered, but not as the person from whom someone could not get away. This is not the moment to share the philosophy behind your new business idea and why it is better than anything in existence. This is the moment to build rapport. This gives you the opportunity to follow up, ask for an appointment, and have a civilized meeting without interruptions.

An encounter at an event is a casual encounter. Networking is not a meeting, a sales call, or a job interview. One thing I can almost promise you: The conversation will be interrupted at least once, if not many times.

Your goal is to connect with the individual sufficiently that you can comfortably follow up and have him or her take your call.

Sophisticated networkers know when to move on. ∼ BOB METCALFE, INVENTOR OF ETHERNET AND FOUNDER OF 3COM

Here are some thoughts to guide you:

- Talk for three to five minutes—a maximum of eight.
- If others are standing nearby, bring them into your conversation.
- Leave before you are left.
- If you want to follow up, say so and ask for a card.
- Be sure to follow up!

DON'T OVERSHARE

Sometimes when we meet people, we feel we have found a long-lost friend. It is so refreshing to connect with someone who understands us and feels our joy (or pain). We laugh together, and we find that the conversation seems too short. Once I met someone socially who said that maybe she should come and get some networking help. By the end of the next drink, I knew about her divorce and her ex-inlaws, that fact that she had been fired from her last job, and her dislike of eating. She shared more information than I could possibly digest, and we had just met. Let your network nurture slowly. You are in there for the long haul.

Summary: Networking is like a fine meal. Slow down and savor the flavors and experience.

8

Places to Network

NETWORKING ON PLANES AND TRAINS

When you are in transit is an optimal time to practice your networking skills. First of all, the person doesn't know you yet, so he or she has no preconceived notions of who you are and how you should behave. Second, you are in public, so if something goes astray, you can get away quickly. Third, something wonderful might happen. Here are some guidelines to help you maximize these situations:

- Carry a book and have it visible. When you first talk to someone, this indicates that you have something else to do and won't necessarily talk his or her ear off. Also, if the person turns out to be boring, you can begin reading right away.
- When you sit down, smile and say hello.
- Ask if he or she is heading to a meeting or heading home (see Bob Metcalfe's sidebar).
- Respect the person's personal space.
- Watch the person's body language—if the person shifts away from you, it's a sign that she or he wants to be left alone.

"Fly First Class"

Bob Metcalfe, inventor of Ethernet and founder of 3Com

These were the first words of wisdom he offered me. For the next hour, he shared tactical networking insights with a spirited sense of humor.

"Arrive at parties early" was another tidbit. He articulated what everyone feels—will anyone come to my party? He explained the value of this time you spend with the host. You can help out with last-minute chores, you learn the name of the dog, you know where the bathrooms are. You ingratiate yourself with the host. "Stay late," he said. "Interesting discussions happen as the party winds down."

He pointed out that this takes confidence because it can feel awkward at first. As people arrive, it is easier to meet them if you are already in the room. Don't be the first to leave, and people who do cameo appearances are "annoying."

Here are some of his other insights:

- Say "hi" at the beginning of the flight. He pointed out that there is an unwritten plane rule that you cannot say "hi" in the middle of the flight.
- On planes, help people with their luggage.
- Respect personal space. Even though he is a tall person, he commented on how awkward it is when someone does not show consideration for that territory.
- Hand-write thank-you notes. If your writing is terrible, print.
- The highest compliment is to ask someone's opinion.
- Email when you don't want anything.
- Make your emails short.
- Extend your hand and introduce yourself.
- Women are nice to talk to; they are curious.
- Like small talk.
- Be interest*ed*.
- Don't see networking as a goal.
- Think of it as tennis: You must always be ready with your racket back.
- Have fun!
- Networking blunder—never ask a woman when the baby's due.

NETWORKING AT CONFERENCES AND TRADE SHOWS

At a trade show, people make up their mind in four seconds whether they will stop at your booth or not.[14] It is always crucial to make a strong first impression, and the stakes are higher at large events such as conferences and trade shows. Everyone on the team must reflect the image and style of the company at all times and in all places. That includes elevators, restaurants, planes, shuttle buses, and hotel lobbies, to name just a few.

Working the Booth

Make a point of catching people's eye when they approach. Smile and say hello. If the person is also an exhibitor, ask a question such as how many shows she or he typically attends in a year or what in particular she or he likes about this one. If the person is an attendee, ask questions about him or her before you do too much talking. Then you will be able to tailor your comments to the individual.

Book Appointments Ahead of Time

In many cases, you are attending because there is someone specific you want to meet with. Make the connection a week or so in advance. Explain why you'd like time together. Be sure to state what problem you can solve. Don't overcommit yourself. You can quickly run out of time, and canceling appointments at shows is not professional.

I was attending a conference, so I read the bios of the speakers a few weeks ahead of time. It turned out that I had an alumni connection with one of them. Even though we hadn't met before, I sent a note mentioning the connection and saying that I'd be at the conference. We emailed a few times and then spoke. It turned out she was looking for a consultant to help on a project. Next thing I knew, I had a paid project that I wouldn't have gotten if I hadn't contacted the speaker beforehand.

So Many Booths, So Little Time!

A show or conference can get overwhelming fast. The challenge is to identify in advance whom you want to see and why. Walk with someone else in the industry who is well known and respected. (Be sure you are not stalking that person—see the section on persistence versus stalking in Chapter 11.)

Conferences can quickly become exhausting. While it's great to be away from the office, rarely does the mind truly shut down. Find a quiet place somewhere—in the convention hall, back at your room, in a restaurant—to gather your thoughts and be alone.

Remember, it's quality contacts that you are after. The number of business cards you get is not an indicator of future business. It's the quality of your interaction with the person who gave you the card that matters.

Get off the show floor. A lot of bonding happens off site. If you are invited to sponsored parties, be sure to attend, say hello to the person who invited you, and thank him or her as you leave.

Table for 20

When you attend a conference or trade show, ask the concierge to book a dinner reservation for 20 at a nearby restaurant for the second evening of the conference. While you are meeting people at the conference, invite them to dinner. It's a great way to introduce people to one another, and you are the one who made it happen.

Before your boss hyperventilates at the idea of signing off on that expense account, this doesn't mean that you need to pick up the tab. You can organize something without paying for it. In fact, mention the name of the restaurant when you invite people and mention the price of a typical entrée. This signals that they are invited to attend, but they are expected to pay their share.

Note: Let the server know in advance that everyone will want some type of an individual receipt, and leave a very generous tip.

Summary: You help everyone avoid the dread of figuring out what to do for dinner in a strange town, you (and your company) gain visibility, and you connect strangers who are at the same conference for similar purposes.

NETWORKING AT JOB FAIRS

This is an excellent opportunity for you to have your ear to the ground and learn about various companies for which you would like to work. You can have conversations with other attendees and with companies

---

"Be Curious"

Frederic D. Rosen, chairman and CEO of Key3Media, producers of Comdex, Next Generation Networks, Interlop, to name just a few conferences

In tight economic times, conference budgets get cut. How does the leader of a company that produces such events compete and make the company's conferences a "must attend"?

Here are the insights from such a person, Fred Rosen:

- All things being equal, people want face-to-face meetings.
- Make it easy for people to meet and interact.
- Have fun.
- Get all the best industry leaders to attend.
- Conferences require social skills, and those can be taught.
- Be curious.
- Don't be phony!
- Learn how to exit from a conversation gracefully—"let's follow up on that later."
- Put interesting people together.
- Be patient.
- Make it comfortable for people to connect.

that are interviewing. You can quickly get a sense of whether the company or the industry is one that you want to be a part of. Consider this valuable research time. Here are some thoughts on how to maximize the job fair experience:

- Dress for the job you want, not the one you have.
- Wear what you would wear if it were an interview—professional attire such as a suit or a coat and tie.
- Look at your feet—do your shoes signal success?
- You have one chance to make a first impression.
- Information interviews are just as important as the "real" one.
- If you don't do well here, you won't be recommended to others.
- Be able to tell your story.
- Study the company's web site.
- Do prep work about those you will be meeting.
- Have a good handshake and good eye contact.
- Smile!
- Stand up straight.
- Have a pen and paper to take notes.
- Treat everyone with respect—don't make any assumptions. I heard the story of a college student who managed to secure an interview at a job fair. He asked a woman from the company for a cup of coffee. As he settled in, he then asked one of the men when the vice president of sales was going to join them. The woman looked at him and said she was the vice president of sales.
- Have a breath mint 15 minutes beforehand.
- Write a handwritten thank-you note immediately. This is to acknowledge their time and ideas, not to pitch them.
- Strike up a conversation with the organizers of the job fair. They know the inside scoop!

"When You're Unemployed, Deploy Your Network"
~ JEFF TAYLOR, FOUNDER AND CHAIRMAN OF MONSTER.COM

"Many people start networking when they are looking for work," he said. "This is a mistake. You shouldn't be creating your network at that time, you should be putting it to work for you."

Jeff Taylor started Monster by himself, and it is now in over 20 countries. This is a fearless man who talks about being parented by those who enjoyed the freedoms of the 1960s and passed that spirit to their son.

Here are some of his comments about networking:

- Always be in networking mode.
- Talk to everyone you meet—there's no excuse not to.
- Ask questions and talk about their interests.
- Be curious and be a very good listener.
- Ask what people do and what they like to do.
- Do a lot of public speaking—he gives 60 to 70 speeches a year.
- Be comfortable in front of others.
- The top thing you can do as a leader to ensure the success of your business is be out there talking to people.
- You never know!
- The first 10 to 15 minutes of any meeting is never about the business topic. Ask questions of those in the meeting. How was your weekend? How are the kids?
- Work for a mission-driven company.
- Bring people together.
- If you are an inconsistent person, your network will reflect that.
- Your network is your halo.
- Have a bunch of hobbies.
- Learning and networking are synonymous.
- The more nervous you are, the more opportunity there is.
- The only way to coast is downhill—don't do it! Work!
- Start—or you won't win.
- Get on boards.
- Create a rich environment for your employees where they can make friends.
- Love being busy! It prevents stress.
- Have a peer group and a group who are senior to you.
- What you do when you're not trying to get people to watch says what and who you really are.

NETWORKING AT MEETINGS

The first few minutes of a meeting are an excellent time to network. The atmosphere is casual, and the conversation is light. Take advantage of the mood and get to know others in the room. While this is written from the perspective of a meeting with outsiders present, the principles can be applied to internal meetings as well. Here are some thoughts:

- Determine who is the note taker. (When in doubt, you should take the notes.)
- Arrive as early as you can. This avoids the angst of walking into a room full of strangers.
- Stand up when you meet someone, shake hands, and maintain good eye contact.
- Exchange business cards at the beginning of the meeting. Place the cards in front of you in the order people sit around the table.
- Ask two or three neutral questions. Some examples include

  - How did you all first meet?
  - Have you done business together before?
  - Where did you work before?

- Write down the names of all attendees on a piece of paper. Or line up their business cards in the order that they are sitting.
- Date the first page and number all pages.
- Have clear "next step" actions written out.
- At the end, go around, thank others for attending, and shake hands.
- If there are people from out of town, make sure they have directions to their next destination.

9

Best Practices

There is nothing that builds confidence more than knowing best practices. When you need to know them isn't the time to learn them. Start now! This has nothing to do with wealth or education; it has everything to do with self-respect.

Look carefully at this section, and keep practicing until you can properly teach someone else. It makes it easier to get things done in life. You can relax and stay focused on your conversation.

Knowing best practices gives us peace of mind that we know how to conduct ourselves. Being familiar with the right thing to do in the right circumstance gives you confidence. Learn it and do it now! Eliminate anything that could get you eradicated from furthering any business relationship you have or want to have.

MANNERS

Your manners are always under examination, and by committees little suspected, awarding or denying you very high prizes when you least think it. ~ RALPH WALDO EMERSON

Manners are both the cake and the icing. Dessert just isn't quite right with only one or the other. You never hear people complain that someone's manners are too good. In fact, when manners are done right, they are invisible. That's the point: There is only an upside to knowing and practicing proper manners. For networking, here are a few highlights:

- *Handshakes.* Both men and women should shake hands. Ladies, some men have been raised to not extend their hand unless you do so first. Therefore, put your hand out and greet the other person.
- *Dining.* If you make the invitation, you select the restaurant. You also should plan to pay. Make advance arrangements with the wait staff to pay for the meal so that this is seamless. Even if the person you are with is on an expense account, you want to acknowledge that they are personally giving you their time.
- *Alcohol.* Don't drink during the day, and be cautious in the evening. Always give up your car keys if requested.
- *Smoking.* Just don't.
- *Conversations.* Discuss, never debate.
- *Flirting.* This is business. Flirt at another time and place.
- *Jokes.* Don't tell any joke you wouldn't want your kids or grandmother to hear (and repeat). This says something about your integrity, too.
- *Invitations.* Respond within five days of *receiving* an invitation.
- *Attire.* Ask the host what is appropriate, and comply.
- *Briefcase.* This wonderful container of your life sits on the subway floor and the trunk and floor of your car, not to mention rest rooms and other places. Don't plop it on a lovely wood conference table or a chair.
- *For gentlemen*: Open doors and walk on the outside of the street. Few men do this anymore, and it will be noticed even if it isn't commented on.

Manners open doors that power, position, and money can-not. Learning the "rules" of business etiquette is easy; they are 80% common sense and 20% kindness. ~ DANA MAY CASPERSON, AUTHOR OF *POWER ETIQUETTE*

THE RECEPTIONIST OR EXECUTIVE ASSISTANT

There is a reason the term *gatekeeper* is used. This person is a pro-tector. If you have one, you know the value of this. If you are work-ing with someone else's, he or she can be your facilitator to success —or your worst enemy. Get the gatekeeper to believe in what you want to accomplish. Be friendly, respectful, and courteous at all times.

If you have a receptionist or executive administrator, here are some reminders:

- Thank him or her frequently.
- Make sure that he or she knows your expectations on how to make people feel welcome.
- This person is your most important ambassador.
- Teach the person how to answer the phone and greet your guests. He or she is your client's first impression of you and your business. How he or she appears, talks, and behaves reflects on you and the company.
- Invest in this person.
- Use the words *please* and *thank you* often when speaking with her or him.
- Have a clear policy about what topics are or are not appro-priate for her or him to discuss with any visitors.
- Also do the same for web surfing in a public setting.
- Have drinks or water nearby.

INTRODUCTIONS

This simple gesture sets the tone of a conversation. It often provides ways to start the conversation as well. How you introduce yourself and others will make them feel connected or rejected. Just as with manners, learn some quick ways to make introductions and feel confident doing so.

Introduce Yourself

It is crucial that you have an introduction you like and can easily say. I've heard some that are quite complicated and overwhelming. Note that an introduction is different from your elevator pitch, which may or may not follow an introduction depending on the circumstances. The elevator pitch is typically around 30 seconds and sounds a bit like a sales pitch. These became quite popular during the "dot-com" days.

Your introduction should invite a conversation and be extremely brief—no more than 5 to 10 seconds at the most. It should include three things:

1. Your name
2. How you fit into the situation
3. Why the other person should care

Use words such as *help, provide, contribute, give, serve, teach,* and *solve.* The introduction is about what you can do for others, not what they can do for you. Your introduction is successful if it invites questions. If it shuts down the conversation, it was unsuccessful, and you need to rework it.

Here are some examples:

- I'm Susan Smith, I'm an exhibitor at this show from People Technology, and we help companies find the right people for their technology positions.
- I'm George Adams, I'm a speaker at the conference, and I help companies identify and execute their marketing strategy.

Here is an example at a meeting:

- I'm John Dunn, I'm in the finance department, and I'm here to help with the business plan.

When you get more comfortable with your introduction, start switching it around. Say your name at the end. The other person is more likely to remember your name if you do. You may want to add something humorous. During one of the training sessions for relationship managers at a bank, a gentleman said he "managed relationships but couldn't help out with the one at home." It got a good laugh and was very memorable.

When men first meet, they immediately introduce themselves. Women sometimes do, but not as frequently.

Summary: In business, you should simply state who you are and say what is your connection to the meeting, event, etc. As much as possible, provide information that will spark a dialogue.

One Size Doesn't Fit All

You need to master a variety of introductions—after all, you have multiple roles. If you are at your child's baseball game, introducing yourself with your title from work would come across as odd, to say the least—as would the opposite, for example, if you were at a conference and you introduced yourself as Jimmy's dad.

Introduce Someone Else

When you are meeting business professionals, you are often called upon to introduce people. This can be a formal introduction or something more casual. Use this opportunity as an excellent way to get conversations started. If the introductions are in a more formal setting, here are some guidelines to follow for the proper order:

- Younger to older
- Junior to senior
- Company employee to guest company individual
- Your executive to customer or client

Other pointers:

- Start with the person's name.
- Then give his or her title or role.
- Give the name of the company (if necessary).
- Mention something that is unique about the person.

Here's a sample introduction: "Susan Jones, I would like you to meet Jack Collins, our vice president of marketing. Jack, this is Susan, our new manager of customer service. Jack is an avid sailor. Susan sails at the MIT Yacht Club."

Names

Using someone's name is important when making introductions. Here are some guidelines.

- Learn what name the person actually uses. For example, is it Richard or Rick, Deborah or Deb?
- Use a nickname only if that is what the person uses in business.
- For unusual pronunciations, practice ahead of time, and don't hesitate to ask the person again. It's better than punting and getting it wrong.
- If someone walks up to you and you should introduce them but you don't remember the names of the people you are with, introduce yourself and then invite the others to introduce themselves.
- See the section in Chapter 10 on how to remember names.

OVERNETWORKING

With so many events available, selecting the right events can seem daunting. In some cases we start "overnetworking," which leads to burnout and then to bad networking experiences. Not a good idea!

This is getting more commonplace and becoming a growing hazard. The incidents of overnetworking are getting more horrifying. When the economy shifted recently, I started receiving calls from people I had met over a year ago and had never heard from since, asking "When can I take you to lunch?" My first thought was, who *are* you?

Overnetworking is avoidable. It happens when we're scared and disorganized. It can easily be fixed with a few changes to your behavior. Before you make a call or attend a networking event, take five minutes and ask yourself a few key questions.

Go back to your contact "Whether Report" (Figure 4-5) and evaluate

- When did I last communicate with this person?
- What were the circumstances?
- Will he or she know me by name?
- What is my ultimate goal in making this call or attending this event?
- How will I determine if the interaction is a success?
- Do I want information, support, a job lead, an introduction, or something else?
- Is this goal written down?

For a phone call to a specific person, ask yourself,

- What am I asking of this person?
- Is it something he or she can do?
- Is this the right person to be asking for help and/or input?

- When he or she called in the past, did I take the call? Did I return it promptly?
- Have I practiced out loud what I want to say?
- Have I written out a list of the things I want to ask this person?
- Have I received permission from the introducer to use his or her name?
- Am I ready to speak right now if this person can give me a few minutes immediately?
- Am I making it easy for this person to help me?
- If he or she wants to schedule an appointment, is my calendar open and do I know my availability?
- If you want to schedule a meeting, suggest some dates and follow up.

For an event, ask yourself

- Is there someone whose opinion I respect and who has attended the event before to advise me whether or not this is worth my time?
- Do I have business cards with me?
- Am I able to confidently introduce myself?
- Have I had a good day, or am I feeling grumpy?
- Have I had a bad hair day? (See the Yale study mentioned in Chapter 4.)
- If I walk into the event and don't get my energy in 10 minutes, will I give myself permission to leave without berating myself?

For a meeting, ask yourself,

- Has the person given me advice before?
- If so, did I follow it? If not, why not? Will I be able to explain it?
- Do I have pen and paper ready to take notes?

- Is my cell phone, pager, or PDA *off*?
- What do I want to have happen afterwards?

Summary: Invest some time in your preparation. You will show up at events that are interesting and worth your while. When you do that, you are typically a happier and more likable person. That will attract people to you and your business.

10

Best Practices When Face to Face

From walking in the door to walking out, this chapter will provide a step-by-step guide to successfully navigate a networking event. Take a look at the "XPlanation" diagram in Figure 10-1. This gives you a visual step-by-step guide.

Wear something that makes you feel confident and will make it easier for someone to describe you. Men can wear a tie with a nice design, and women can wear a suit in a color other than navy, brown, or black.

Before you head to an event, conference, or meeting, you need to pack your Networking Survival Kit. The purpose is to have everything you need for networking in one place. When you head out the door, you can grab the kit and everything is stocked and ready to go.

PACKING LIST FOR NETWORKING SURVIVAL KIT

The idea behind packing your Networking Survival Kit[15] is to ensure that you have everything you need or want readily at hand. There's nothing worse than realizing you've left behind your business cards or you don't have a pen. Just as in the previous discussion on best

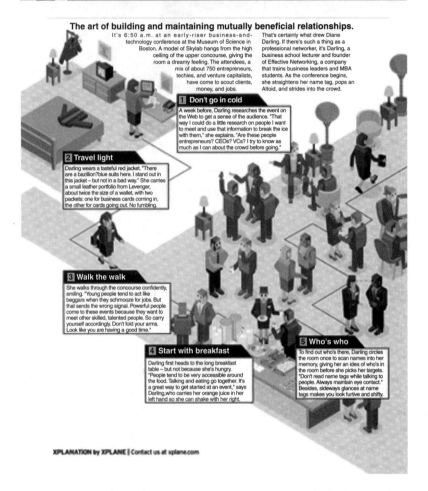

Figure 10-1   XPLANATION

Source: XPLANE (xplane.com). First appeared in *MBA Jungle Magazine*, Mar/Apr 2002.

practices, make it easy and less stressful on yourself. Have this kit ready to go. You may wish to pack several—one for your briefcase, another for the car, and one for your office. If there is some wonderful product or tool we missed, send an email to Info@ EffectiveNetworking.com.

Kit for an Event, Conference, Trade Show or Meeting

- Your business cards.
- Two business card cases, one for your cards and the other for

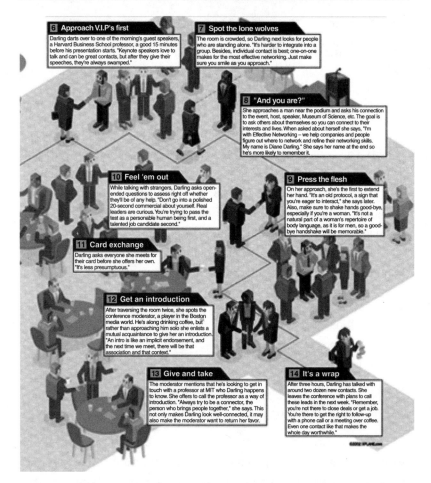

6 Approach V.I.P.'s first

Darling darts over to one of the morning's guest speakers, a Harvard Business School professor, a good 15 minutes before his presentation starts. "Keynote speakers love to talk and can be great contacts, but after they give their speeches, they're always swamped."

7 Spot the lone wolves

The room is crowded, so Darling next looks for people who are standing alone. "It's harder to integrate into a group. Besides, individual contact is best; one-on-one makes for the most effective networking. Just make sure you smile as you approach."

8 "And you are?"

She approaches a man near the podium and asks his connection to the event, host, speaker, Museum of Science, etc. The goal is to ask others about themselves so you can connect to their interests and lives. When asked about herself she says, "I'm with Effective Networking – we help companies and people figure out where to network and refine their networking skills. My name is Diane Darling." She says her name at the end so he's more likely to remember it.

10 Feel 'em out

While talking with strangers, Darling asks open-ended questions to assess right off whether they'll be of any help. "Don't go into a polished 20-second commercial about yourself. Real leaders are curious. You're trying to pass the test as a personable human being first, and a talented job candidate second."

9 Press the flesh

On her approach, she's the first to extend her hand. "It's an old protocol, a sign that you're eager to interact," she says later. Also, make sure to shake hands good-bye, especially if you're a woman. "It's not a natural part of a woman's repertoire of body language, as it is for men, so a good-bye handshake will be memorable."

11 Card exchange

Darling asks everyone she meets for their card before she offers her own. "It's less presumptuous."

12 Get an introduction

After traversing the room twice, she spots the conference moderator, a player in the Boston media world. He's along drinking coffee, but rather than approaching him solo she enlists a mutual acquaintance to give her an introduction. "An intro is like an implicit endorsement, and the next time we meet, there will be that association and that context."

13 Give and take

The moderator mentions that he's looking to get in touch with a professor at MIT who Darling happens to know. She offers to call the professor as a way of introduction. "Always try to be a connector, the person who brings people together," she says. This not only makes Darling look well-connected, it may also make the moderator want to return her favor.

14 It's a wrap

After three hours, Darling has talked with around two dozen new contacts. She leaves the conference with plans to call these leads in the next week. "Remember, you're not there to close deals or get a job. You're there to get the right to follow-up with a phone call or a meeting over coffee. Even one contact like that makes the whole day worthwhile."

the cards you receive. I suggest both be classy—they can perhaps inspire a conversation.

- Pen, either one that is memorable or one that you can lose.
- Note cards—start with 3 × 5 cards or a small notebook.
- Sharpie marker—for your name badge.
- Breath mints—a must!
- Directions to the event.
- Printout of the front page of the hosting organization's web site.

- Printout of the staff and board members for the organization.

For a meeting, add

- Portfolio for taking notes.
- Copies of the personal snapshots of everyone who will be in the meeting.

If you arrive without what you need, you will come across as apathetic and uninterested. It's amazing how many people show up for meetings without a pen and paper. Curiously, it's often the CEOs who have both and the junior people who don't. *Think like a CEO!* Be ready to accept help and share information.

While your business cards and other networking tools are important, so are the intangible networking tools. Be sure to pack these as well:

- Smile
- Tall posture
- Positive attitude
- Curiosity
- Sense of humor

Networking Survival Kit for the Office   There is nothing worse than getting ready to head to an event or a meeting and realizing that you have dog hair on your suit coat or that your hem has come out. Put together a small kit for your drawer at work and/or your car.

- Toothbrush and paste
- Hand lotion
- Nail file, clippers, and/or polish
- Comb and/or brush
- Hair spray
- Lint brush
- Cosmetics/shaving kit
- Tissues

- Socks/hosiery
- Moist towelettes—see the resource guide for some ones we've tried out
- Breath mints
- Safety pins
- Sewing kit

NAME BADGES OR NAVEL DECORATIONS?

I'm not talking about military brass—I'm talking about your belly button. While the badge holders with long straps have advantages (e.g., they don't puncture your clothes), it is extremely uncomfortable talking to someone whose eyes keep dropping to read the name tag in that *personal* territory.

Women who place their name badge south of their shoulder and north of their waist are asking for attention to an area they otherwise would not want focused on. Here are some basics:

- Name badges aren't for you, they are for the other person.
- Carry a Sharpie marker.
- When you arrive at an event, print your name in large letters instead of using the ballpoint pen at the registration desk. The person who may give you business or a job just might be over 40.
- If you're gutsy, add something memorable. For example, suppose you are a relationship manager at a bank. Here's your name tag: "Dan, the Dr. Phil of Business Banking." It's guaranteed to start a conversation.
- Name badges go on your right shoulder. (Left is for the Pledge of Allegiance.) Why the right side? When you shake hands, the eye naturally travels up the right arm. Make it easy for the person and don't force them to do a "chest scan" to read your name. Put your name badge high on your shoulder so that people can look in your eyes when they greet you.

Summary: Your name badge is a tool for others to learn and remember your name. Make it easy (and professional) for them to do so.

HANDSHAKE

Your handshake communicates a powerful nonverbal message before you speak. A firm handshake conveys confidence, assurance, interest and respect. A limp handshake can send the opposite message. ~ DANA MAY CASPERSON

Have you ever received a bad handshake? Ah! There is the vice grip handshake, and then there are the people who prefer to slap a dead fish in your palm.

You want people to remember *you*, not your handshake. Your handshake is one of the most important communication tools you have. Use it to your advantage. You want to communicate that you are friendly, you can get things done, and you know how to conduct yourself in a business situation. You do not want to communicate that you are aloof, uncertain of your abilities, unprofessional, or on a power trip.

I was working with a female senior executive who was looking for a job. At the end of our first session, I went to shake her hand and say good-bye. Her handshake was terrible! Here she was seeking an executive-level role, and her handshake felt like she was in elementary school. I asked her to shut the door. She knew immediately. She said, "I have a bad handshake, don't I?"

We practiced handshakes a few times, and when I met her the next time, she was all smiles. She told me that she went home that night and told her husband that she had a bad handshake. He commented that he wasn't sure they had ever shaken hands. What a surprise! Most husbands and wives don't shake hands, and that's just fine! He agreed, her handshake wasn't good. Over the next week, she practiced as much as she possibly could and gained confidence in the process.

Good handshakes are easy to learn. What's important is that you have someone who is honest with you. Typically I wear a ring on my right hand. If there is a dent in my skin in the shape of the ring I'm wearing, then the handshake is too strong. When I show the person the physical remnant of their handshake, they are really surprised and appreciative that someone has told them.

No one wants to offend another person. However, letting someone repeat behavior that diminishes his or her chance of success isn't helping that person, it's hurting him or her. The key is to communicate your message carefully.

Use this book as an excuse to tell someone about the importance of handshakes. Ask this person to test yours. What does the person like about it? What doesn't feel right? Do this with people of both gender. Also test your handshake with people who are in their 60s or older. You don't want to crush anyone's fragile bones.

"Handshaking, Gender, Personality, and First Impressions"[16] is a formal study that was conducted at the University of Alabama Department of Psychology. It was written up in the July 2000 issue of the *Journal of Personality and Social Psychology.*

It states, "a firm handshake was related positively to extraversion and emotional expressiveness and negatively to shyness and neuroticism." In some cases, it isn't until the handshake and introduction that we have had a chance to utter a single word to the other person. The smile may be welcoming, and then, yuck—a dead fish handshake. Let several people in your business network know that you are reading this book and ask them to critique your handshake.

History of Handshake

The handshake started in medieval times when people who met would look at the other's right hand to see if there was a weapon in it. To signify trust, they would stretch out their right hand, indicating that it was safe to approach.

Characteristics of a Handshake

Today, in most cases, shaking hands isn't life-threatening. However, there are many people out there who were never taught a proper handshake. The University of Alabama study concluded that there was indeed a relationship between the characteristics of a handshake (strength, vigor, completeness of grip, duration, and eye contact) and a positive first impression.

Note: This information is applicable for doing business in the United States. In other countries and cultures, however, there are other greetings that are appropriate. It is recommended that you research the local customs prior to traveling.

A handshake is straightforward. Here's how it works:

- Look at your right hand. Notice the skin between your thumb and your index finger. It's soft and webby, just like a duck's webbed foot. This part of your hand should touch the other person's right hand. Think, web touching web or thumb aiming at thumb.
- Next, the palms of the hands should touch lightly. You don't want to cup your hand. This makes people wonder what you are hiding inside.
- Finally, shake up and down slightly or hold for a moment and then . . . *Let go*! It's amazing how many people forget that part.
- Maintain eye contact throughout the handshake and introduction.
- After the handshake, ask yourself, do I remember the color of his or her eyes? This is a good test of whether or not you have paid attention during the introduction.
- A reminder: Ladies, extend your hand. In business, it's a signal of confidence and equality.

Handshakes to Avoid

Here are some frequently used, and sometimes misused, handshakes.

Bill Clinton Handshake   Many have the image of our fine former president shaking hands with his right hand while placing his left on the person's shoulder. This should be done only if the two parties know each other quite well. Men should use caution if they do it to women, especially women they don't know. In other words, ask your attorney first. Touching above the elbow can be grounds for a sexual harassment claim.

Churchlady Handshake   This is when someone puts his or her left hand on top of the two right ones that are shaking, as if to say, "Aren't you cute, dear, so nice to see you." Handshakes are between two hands, not three.

"I'm in Charge" Handshake   These people aren't quite sure they are in charge, so just to make sure, while shaking hands, they rotate their hand ever so slightly so that theirs is on top. This subtle messages says, "I'm superior."

"What Year Did You Graduate?"   This is for the people who lost an arm-wrestling contest at summer camp and have been trying to recover ever since. While shaking your hand, they grip so tightly that their graduation year, so delicately engraved on their class ring, is now permanently embedded in the side of your finger. Most likely they mean no harm, and they also have no clue as to how strong they are.

Men Shake and Women Kiss—What to Do?

During a recent discussion on this topic, an accomplished professional mentioned that he was teaching his 8-year-old son to shake hands, but he wasn't teaching his 10-year-old daughter.

Men shake hands all the time. Just watch them. They say hello with a handshake, and they also say good-bye with one. They say congratulations with a handshake. This is true in a social setting or a professional one.

Women have not been raised to shake hands when they see each other in business or social settings. Men who have been brought up with traditional manners have been told not to put their hand out until the woman does. In a business setting, gender should not matter—everyone should shake hands with everyone else.

Summary: A firm handshake signals confidence and the ability to get things done.

HOW TO REMEMBER NAMES

My memory is so bad that many times I forget my own name. ~ DON QUIXOTE

You've just met someone, and less than a second later you have no idea what the person's name is. This is often one of the most embarrassing and awkward moments in networking. With a few techniques, you can reverse this painful instant and come across as polished and professional. A person's name is melodic to his or her ears, use it. I have yet to meet a single person who has not had his or her name misspelled or even been called by the wrong name completely. It happens no matter how simple or complex our name is.

Ask yourself, would I pay more attention to someone's name if I knew that when I walked out of here, I would get a new client, a donation for my nonprofit, or a new job?

Here are some helpful ways to remember names:

- *Think of $100 per name.* Remember Benjamin Franklin and the "club for mutual improvement"? His face graces the $100 bill. If I promised to give you a $100 bill for each name you remembered, would you try harder? My guess is that you would indeed get a number of names right. Whatever motivates you to learn names, do it! Really try!

- *Get it right the first time.* When someone introduces him- or herself and you haven't heard the name or can't say it, simply ask the person to repeat it.

- *Spell it back.* This shows that you are genuinely interested in getting it right.

- *Use the name.* In the first few sentences, use the person's name once or twice. Don't do it too often, or it appears pretentious and can quickly become annoying.

- *Ask a question.* If you know someone else with the same name, ask if there is a relation. Or ask what the derivation of the name is. We have become so politically correct that we don't want to offend anyone; on the other hand, we're willing to walk around mispronouncing someone's name (assuming we heard it to begin with).

- *Connect the name to something.* If you know someone with the same name, make a mental note of the connection. For example, I used to work with someone named Susan Fleming —just like Ian Fleming who wrote the Bond books. Remember whom he or she is with when you meet and make the connection to that person.

  - Be cautious about your word association. When I was teaching, someone shared this story with me. There was someone named Chip, and he couldn't remember the nickname, especially since it was for a woman. So he thought of his favorite chip—a chocolate chip cookie. The next time he saw her, he smiled and said, "Hi, Cookie!"

- *Write the name down.* When you are in a meeting and people are introducing themselves, pull out a piece of paper and write each person's name with a few words.

- *Use tent cards.* If you are hosting a meeting, provide tent cards. Bring an $8^{1}/_{2} \times 11$ piece of paper, fold it lengthwise, and use it as a tent card. Construction paper works just fine.

- *Create a system that works for you.* If you remember things visually, mentally write the person's name down. If you are an auditory person, say it out loud. If you are a kinesthetic learner, write it with your toe in the carpet or image it in the sky.

- *Make it easy for others.* If for whatever reason—logical or not —others don't get your name right, take responsibility and when you introduce yourself, make it easy. Typically I say, "I'm Diane Darling—just like sweetheart." If someone is writing it down, I'll add, "That's Diane with one *n*." Other people are not intentionally trying to clobber your name. However, they may be nervous, confused, tired—who knows. Make them feel better by helping them out.

Summary: Saying someone's name gets that person's attention. When you have someone's attention, you can build rapport and make a personal connection.

FOOD AND BEVERAGE

This is network, not net-eat! ~ AUTHOR

Most networking events involve eating in some fashion, whether it's a breakfast meeting, a cocktail party, or a sit-down dinner. We can quickly become distracted by the food and forget why we are attending in the first place. If you have to eat as a part of the event, then do so. Otherwise, consider having a snack before you head out so that you can focus on your conversation, not your stomach.

Pick Your Priorities—Muffin or Money

Early one morning, I drove to Cape Cod to attend a forum for entrepreneurs and investors. I'm not particularly a morning person, but I had a business idea I wanted to get funded. This was just such an opportunity.

As I scrambled to get out the door, I decided to forgo breakfast, since there would certainly be food at the event. I drove for 90 minutes and arrived shortly after 7 A.M. By this time my brain was wide awake and so was my stomach.

I checked in and headed to grab a glass of juice and a muffin. At that very moment, a conversation began about my brilliant business idea and what capital would be required to get it off the ground. The dialogue was very engaging, and this individual, himself an investor, wanted to make some introductions on my behalf. We walked a few steps as I attempted to juggle the juice glass and muffin as well as a briefcase. As I put my hand out to greet the person I was being introduced to, the muffin lost.

I stood there as animated as Mount Rushmore as I watched the muffin roll down the hall. What I had forgotten that morning was to select a priority. Was it food or appearing professional in front of an investor? The entire situation could have been avoided if I had gotten up a few extra minutes early and had a bite at home or taken a nutrition bar with me and eaten in the car.

> *Summary: Determine what your priority is and give it your full attention. And always eat before you arrive at a stand-up event—no matter what the hour.*

Munch with Your Networking Buddy

If I arrive hungry, I find someone I know well, preferably someone whom I see frequently in business or who is a friend. This is a networking opportunity for both of us; therefore, eating to the side and a quick hello wouldn't be considered rude. I explain my predicament and suggest that we each get a plate of food and a drink and head off to a corner where we can talk and eat. Never make this person feel used. Be sure it is someone whom you see often and whose calls you return immediately and vice versa. Catch up on some pertinent news and then agree that after 5 to 10 minutes, it's time for both of you to get up and move around the room.

How to Juggle a Glass and Plate of Hors d'Oeuvres

First, I strongly suggest you choose one or the other and not juggle. You will feel more confident and that puts those around you at ease. If you must juggle, be very careful. Here are some guidelines:

- Stand near a table so that you can put your glass down frequently.
- Hold your glass in your left hand. Cold drinks in glasses and cans will sweat. If you are holding the drink in your right hand and you reach out to shake hands, you will give the other person a cold, clammy handshake. Or you will have to do a "hip-slap handshake" by wiping off the drink sweat on your clothes prior to shaking hands.

- When drinking white wine, hold your glass by the stem. This keeps your hand from warming the drink.
- Maintain eye contact when talking with someone.
- If you drop something in someone's home, pick it up immediately.
- If you are at a function, use your best judgment.
- Purchase a Party Clip that clips on your plate and has a ring to hold the wine glass (www.PartyClip.com).

"I Drink to Make Others More Interesting"

Networking frequently includes a bar. Today it is more socially acceptable not to drink at all, or at least to drink less. Whatever your tolerance is, know it and follow it. Some people get sleepy if they are tired and have a glass of wine on an empty stomach. You want to be unforgettable; however, there are some memories that are better than others.

Here are some thoughts:

- Carry a snack in your briefcase, so that it's easy to have a few bites before you start drinking.
- Alternate one alcoholic drink and one glass of water.
- Have a glass of seltzer with a splash of wine rather than the opposite.
- Consider stopping at two alcoholic drinks.
- If you don't drink, find a moment to tell the bartender what you prefer.
- Eat. This may sound simple, but it is easy to overlook. If you are hungry, don't risk your health or well-being by not getting some nourishment. Consider snacking ahead of time or having a nutrition bar in your briefcase so that you are focused on networking, not your stomach.
- Give up your car keys if they are requested.
- If you are in a home with light-colored carpet, stay with white wine or light-colored drinks.

Drinking from the Can

The reason you shouldn't do this isn't just because of manners. If you, or someone you know, did a stint working in a supply room while you were in college, you may remember that in addition to the stacks of canned goods, there were also critters, and their remnants. Clean off the top of a soda or beer can and pour it into a glass—if not for you, then for those who are watching who may have had such a summer job.

> *Summary: Networking—either social or business—is about making connections with others for either personal or professional reasons. Drinking can be a part of that. Know your audience and know yourself. Be appropriate and comfortable.*

BUSINESS CARDS—QUALITY VERSUS QUANTITY!

I actually went to a networking event where a game called business card Olympics was played. The idea was to get as many cards as possible during a set time. It was miserable. I was quite sure that not everyone there wanted my card, and vice versa. If I only wanted names, I could buy a list.

One quality conversation makes an event worthwhile, in my opinion. In some cases it's with a person I've met before, but we haven't done business together. Stick to your core goal of meeting people you can add value to and vice versa. Remember: It's quality, not quantity that counts.

AVOID CONVERSATIONS IN PUBLIC PLACES

There are reporters in elevators, sitting next to you at breakfast or in sessions, or standing in restrooms. There are also your competitors. Do *not* engage in any conversation in public that you do not wish to read about the next day in the paper or say anything that your CEO would rather your competitor not know. You don't want to be the one to disclose trade secrets.

HOW TO MEET THE SPEAKER OR A VIP

Often we attend a meeting, event, or conference so that we can meet the speaker or a VIP who is also attending the session. After the person speaks, there is often a crowd and it is all but impossible to meet him or her. If you do truly want to meet such a person, first be sure that you have a specific goal. For example, you want to tell the speaker how much you like his book or to find out who in her company makes purchasing decisions on computers.

Consider approaching the person before he or she speaks. This means you need to do some research in advance of the event. Go to the person's web site and read the bio. Come up with a few questions you can ask. This way, if you find yourself in the elevator with the speaker prior to the presentation, you have a few moments to make a connection.

Only speak for a few minutes. If your goal is to get a meeting, then say so, explain why the person should make time for you, and move on. During a presentation, someone said that he wanted to meet the chairman of a large company. When he was asked for a few more details, it became clear that the chairman wasn't the right person at all. It is easy to think that the person at the top is the only one who can help you. In fact, ask who is the right person. This sends a message of respect and indicates that you are a true professional.

TALK TO PEOPLE WHO ARE ALONE

We all remember that feeling in high school when we were new and didn't know whom to talk to. Now that we are adults, only the scene is different, and for some the feelings are just as painful. Approach people who are on their own. Before too long you can quickly form your own group that is having a brilliant conversation.

If the discussion is less thrilling than you'd like, consider it as a great chance to practice some new skills. In many cases it is the first time the person has been to an event with the hosting organization. Introduce him or her to someone who is involved with the association. It gives you a chance to increase your visibility as well.

GET AN INTRODUCTION

If there is someone at the event that you specifically want to meet, find someone who can introduce you. This makes the entire situation less awkward. Consider sending an email in advance to the person you would like to make the introduction. Articulate what you can offer the other person.

The Rolling Stones were featured on the September 30, 2002, cover of *Fortune*.[17] It turns out that their manager, Michael Cohl, is a very good networker. First of all, he knew his goal. Cohl "would produce new streams of revenue by selling skyboxes, bus tours, TV deals, and taking merchandise to a new level. He would bring in corporate sponsors like Volkswagen and Tommy Hilfiger."

Second, he knew who could help him execute the deal, Prince Rupert. But there was one problem: He didn't know the prince. So he networked until he found someone who did, and that was the band members from Pink Floyd. He called them and asked for an introduction.

Now before you pick up the phone and start asking for introductions, here's why Prince Rupert returned Cohl's call. When Rupert got the message from Pink Floyd, he trusted their judgment. He called Cohl and heard a compelling offer: "$40 million for 40 shows."

If you are in college and beginning your first job search, it is fine to ask for an information interview. However, later in life, you need to do your homework and learn as much as you possibly can about the other person. When the introduction is made, the person already wants to meet you.

When you are at an event and a chance presents itself, quickly ask yourself if this will be your only opportunity to meet the other person. Be strategic, but don't be foolish. You want to come across as poised and polished, not ill prepared or opportunistic.

ASK WHAT YOU CAN DO FOR PEOPLE

When you meet someone you like and want to help, ask that person what you can do for him or her. (See Chapter 12 in order to learn how to ask for help.) I find just asking enhances the rapport with the other person. If you offer, be sure you do it. It is of little benefit to your reputation if you make offers and do not follow up.

FOLLOW UP

At the end of the XPlane document (see Figure 10-1), you see a "Lego-Diane" walking out with business cards. This is where the rubber hits the road. Few people follow up at all and even fewer know *how* to follow up. This is so important that it has its own chapter in the book. Read Chapter 11 carefully. If you fail to follow up, you have done yourself, your company, or your organization a serious disservice.

HOW TO RUN A NETWORKING EVENT OR MEETING

Much of *The Networking Survival Guide* is focused on you as the attendee or initiator of a networking situation. In many cases, you and your company will be expected to host events rather than attend. This can be a fabulous moment for you and your firm to shine. It can also be your worst nightmare if a competent person isn't responsible for each detail.

It's risky to assume that your executive assistant can double as a meeting planner unless he or she has been specifically trained in this. Consider outsourcing the meeting or having your assistant work with someone in your organization who has handled events before. Some firms have a meeting planning department. Get in touch with this department as early as possible and let it take care of all the event details.

When you work with a professional meeting planning department or firm, you can stay focused on your business needs and someone else can handle the details of the meeting. I contacted Meeting Planners International (MPI) for some suggestions. Here are some thoughts from the recent president of the New England chapter, Todd Bidwell, who also runs Cooper Productions.

- *Hire a meeting planner who understands the importance of strategy*. It is important that the planner understand the goals, the audience, the history of past event successes and failures, the budget parameters, and the client's expectations.

- *Clearly define the goals and objectives of the event.* Defining these expectations will ensure that you focus the proper amount of attention on the appropriate event elements. Your return on investment (ROI) is an important outcome of the event that will be determined by measurable goals.

- *Select a location that will appeal to your attendees.* The event location will make or break your event, for a couple of reasons. Whether you choose to hold your event in a hotel, a museum, a boat, or a historic mansion, the location should reflect the type of event you wish to create and should be desirable to your guests.

- *Remember to leave time for networking.* Too often, enthusiasm for creating the event gets the better of you, and you pack too much into a short period of time. Leave ample time for guests to meet and mingle with one another over drinks or food, or follow a stage presentation with a networking reception.

- *Help others to meet one another.* One of the best ways to assist people in networking with one another is to have members of your event team or staff, assist in the person-to-person introductions.[18]

I have great respect for the myriad of details that meeting planners manage. From my experience attending many functions, here are a few key thoughts:

- Hold a pre-event meeting. Schedule a time when everyone who will be at the event can get together. Be sure that everyone knows the purpose of the event, who the attendees are, and what is expected of company representatives.

- Discuss expected employee behavior. It's ridiculous to attend a hosted event and find clusters of employees whispering and frantically hanging onto each other as if they were in high school. Your employees must be confident and capable of walking up to anyone and representing the company. If they don't know someone, they should introduce themselves and indicate their role in the organization. If they can't do this, send them home. They will damage your firm's reputation.

- Teach handshakes.
- Be sure everyone who is at the event knows and can say what the company does and whom you serve.
- Review what is considered confidential information. Use some examples: "If someone at the party asks what our sales to date are, introduce them to Jeff Smith in sales and he can answer the question."
- Remove confidential information from walls. An event attendee told me she once went to a competitor's party and saw the quarterly numbers on a wall chart.
- Have name badges printed ahead of time. Place them in alphabetical order facing the guests. Be sure they are readable. Do not use the ones that hang around someone's neck, forcing people to "belly button scan" for names.
- Serve food that is easy to eat standing up.
- Create buffer time in the schedule for people to relax, make phone calls, and check email.
- Be sure it is clear who will follow up with leads. For about three months after attending an event, I had two to three people from the same company calling me. It was never clear why each person was calling. The only thing that was clear was that they were each on commission.
- If you cannot afford a meeting planner, send yourself or your assistant to a class.
- Hosting a meeting? Familiarize yourself with Robert's Rules of Order.[19]

11

Follow-Up Techniques

Networking is a recurring commitment.
~ PAM ALEXANDER, *Alexander & Ogilvy*

The difference between successful networking and unsuccessful networking is follow-up. Few do this at all, much less well. Follow-up means that you are interested in further developing a positive relationship for both parties. It is also important that you imagine yourself on the other side of the table. When people follow up with you, answer their request or call. None of us likes to say no to anyone, however, when we return someone's calls even if we don't have the answer that person wants, we are sending a signal that we are a professional who treats others well.

This chapter will provide techniques, resources, technology short cuts, and much more. It will cover how to follow up by email, voicemail, and snail mail, and which one to use when.

THE DIFFERENCE BETWEEN PERSISTENCE AND STALKING

While the difference is subtle, once someone falls into the stalking category, it can be difficult if not impossible to maneuver back.

- Persistence is perseverance, determination, and resolution.
- Stalking is pestering, annoying, aggravating; a synonym can even be persecution.

While it is admirable when people are enthusiastic about working with us or providing services and products, it is unnerving when they cross that invisible line. Instead of being someone we would like to work with in the future, this person shifts to being a part of a network of people to avoid.

Esther Dyson, author and chair of ED Ventures, a global information service company, shared a story. When she was at a trade show in Las Vegas, she was swimming laps. At the end of her lane was someone who had come to the pool and was waiting for her. He strongly suggested that she stop by his company's booth at the show.

This type of behavior can quickly lead to the demise of a professional or personal relationship. At that point, it is best to let go, note the lessons learned, and start over.

It is easy to be persistent without stalking. Here are some techniques.

WHICH METHOD TO USE WHEN

- Use email when time is absolutely of the essence, but your voice/tone isn't. For example, you are giving someone directions for a meeting the next day.
- Use voicemail when the energy of your voice is important. Or if by chance there was a misunderstanding, the kind tone of your voice made it less of a problem.
- You can *never* go wrong using snail mail. I've never heard anyone complain about receiving a handwritten thank-you

note. Of course, the contents may have been too pushy—for example, it was sent with an unrequested brochure.

- Ask the person what he or she prefers when you follow up. Some people definitely have a preference. Use that method!

"CAN I BUY YOU LUNCH?"

If you invite someone to lunch, be clear about what you want. If you are looking for advice or you want to tap into the person's expertise, it may not be the best approach. In essence, you are buying an hour or more of consulting time for about $20. Unless you know the individual well, it can come across as presumptuous and almost insulting. I've had clients share horror stories with me about someone inviting them to lunch and then expecting to split the bill.

Time with a decision maker is so valuable that Nancy Michaels, founder of Impression Impact, recently bid $1000 to have lunch with the CEO of Office Depot.[20] Here are some excerpts from the press release about her experience.

"It was important for me to meet Mr. Nelson," said Michaels. "I wanted to assess his interest in small business seminars. . . . Was it a risk? Absolutely."

> *Summary: Time expires—once spent, it's gone. People guard it carefully and value it highly. If you do so as well, your networking efforts will be recognized, appreciated, and reciprocated.*

IF NOT LUNCH, WHAT TO ASK FOR?

Give someone an option that he or she can say yes to (and make it easy to do so). For example, suggest coffee for 15 minutes at the person's office. He or she is more likely to be able to fit you into the calendar, not to mention that her or his assistant and phone are nearby. On occasions, the person I'm visiting has picked up the phone and immediately introduced me.

Let the person know why you want to meet and what you are asking for. You will significantly increase your chances of getting his or her time and attention. Once I emailed someone and asked if he knew a certain person and would be willing to make an introduction. He wrote back and said of course he knew this person, but he needed to know why I wanted to contact the other person before he would use his connections.

MAKE IT POSSIBLE, AND COMFORTABLE, FOR THE PERSON TO SAY NO

While most of us don't like the word *no*, it does provide an answer. If the person feels that he or she can say no, he or she will respect you. When you ask for something in the future, that will be duly remembered. Say thank you and move on.

AFTER YOU'RE INTRODUCED

If someone made an introduction on your behalf and the person you have been introduced to is not returning calls, here are some tips on what to do next.

- Call the person who made the introduction and let her or him know that you are not getting a response.
- Ask for advice on what the next steps should be.
- Always update that person on the status. It's polite, it makes the person feel appreciated, and it gives you a valid excuse to be in touch.

THREE STRIKES AND YOU'RE OUT

I'm frequently asked how many times someone should follow up. Switch places and ask yourself how many times you want someone to contact you. You want to be known as someone who is respectful and businesslike.

- *Before* you follow up, be sure you know what is the best way to connect with the person.
- Rarely do I follow up more than three times.
- More frequently I start out with both an email and a phone call with a clear, thoughtful, organized message. (See the section on voicemail in Chapter 12.)
- Script both messages and practice your voicemail message out loud.
- Be prepared to have a conversation if the person answers the phone. Sometimes we hide behind technology—don't. Be ready to ask for the business, contribution, or job.
- Write an attention-getting subject line.
- Last, I go back to the person who made the introduction or I leave a third voicemail message.
- Sometimes people do reject us, but they forget to tell us. Well, they actually do tell us, but they do it in their own way. They don't return our call or respond to our email.

PHONE CALLS

The other day I picked up the phone and the person said his name. Then he said, "Here's the information you requested." At that point, I knew I was in trouble. For the life of me I couldn't remember what was the connection between the name and the information I had asked for. I had no choice—I pleaded the fifth. It turned out that he was helping me reach a decision maker at his company.

I'm flattered that people think I have a steel-trap memory. When you follow up, make it easy for the person whom you are calling to remember who you are.

- State your name and the name of your company.
- Jog the person's memory for just one moment. For example, "Diane, this is George Smith from Jones and Company. You asked me to help you meet someone at Smith and Company

who purchases consulting services. I recently met John Sinclair, vice president of marketing, and he's your person!"

- Ask if the person has a moment to talk.
- Provide the information, thank the person, and hang up.

Summary: Proper follow-up can lead to a successful long-term business or personal relationship. Improper follow-up will guarantee that your efforts now and in the future will likely be wasted.

12

Best Practices When Not Face to Face

When we are networking, either we are face to face or we are using some form of technology, be it the phone, email, or letter. Given what you know now about the power of body language, it is always preferable to be with the person. Your goal should be to get your "face in the place" whenever possible. However, that isn't always possible. Here are some techniques to help you maximize networking opportunities when being there just isn't an option.

PHONE

"More than 75% of new contacts make their decision about whether or not to do further business with you during the initial phone call."[21]

Here are some guidelines for making calls:

- Know what you want and what you are going to say or ask before the person answers the phone.
- Script your message.
- Rehearse it—out loud!

- Smile when you call.
- Whenever possible, try and get the person "live" rather than leaving a voicemail message.

Here are some guidelines for receiving calls:

- Answer calls by the third ring (at the latest).
- Smile when you answer the phone.
- Write down the caller's name immediately.
- Be available. I called a company that has a system where you say your name and then the person either takes the call or doesn't. After a few times, I could only assume that the person either didn't really work there or was avoiding my calls. Of course if someone doesn't take your call, you feel rejected. Be present!
- Return calls within 48 hours.
- Use the person's name during the call.
- Make notes when you talk.
- Stand up if you have a problem paying attention.
- Turn your back to your computer.
- Thank the person for calling.

Here's a fun story about a decision made by someone who understood how you come across on the phone. Sheila loved to talk to people and was excellent at her job. I mentioned that I had a new client for her. As I was on the phone, he walked by, so I said I'd transfer the call and connect them. "*No!*" she said. "I'm not dressed right." I laughed and said, "You must be kidding—you're on the phone." She explained that she feels better about herself when she is dressed in business attire, and at the moment she was in jeans. It wasn't how she wanted to "meet" a potential new customer.

Summary: Are you dressed for your call?

Voicemail

Once, when I listened to my voicemail, there was a message with a name I didn't know. The phone number was said so fast that only "Rain Man" could have figured it out. He also gave his email address (spoken as fast as a NFL pass as well). The more I hit replay, the more aggravated I got. I never did figure out the phone number or email address. Instead, I had to call his boss to find out what was going on, which was aggravating for everyone.

We are networking all the time. Each time we connect with someone, we are either reinforcing the positive image he or she has of us or beginning to contribute to his or her impression that we may not be that brilliant after all.

> *Summary: Learn how to leave voicemail. This is a communication tool that can provide a positive image to the recipient or a negative one. The choice is yours. Practice your message. If you can review it before finalizing, do so.*

Before you call or email, take a brief moment to ask yourself if the call is necessary. Are you calling because it is easier to ask someone else to do your work? One time I got a call from someone asking for the phone number of a company. Whether or not this was true, she came across as lazy.

> *Summary: Before you pick up the phone to ask a data question, try to find the information elsewhere. Make contact with someone when you are providing information, not asking for something you already have or can get elsewhere.*

How to Leave a Voicemail Message

Voicemail is a reality in our world. The technology is not going to go away. Learn to make it your friend and an effective networking tool. What happens is that we naturally get nervous, get tongue-tied, and ramble.

Prepare

- Write down what you want to say. It doesn't need to be word for word; even bullet points will help you.
- If you tend to get nervous, write CALM DOWN on the index card and breathe.
- Because I know I can talk fast, I often write, "S-L-O-W D-O-W-N" on the piece of paper.
- Make a connection with the other person in the message as early as possible. Here are some things to be sure you say:
  - Who referred you
  - The purpose of the call
  - Your name
  - Your phone number and/or email address
  - The best time or way to reach you
  - Your name and contact information again

Practice   Going back to *West Wing*, the reason why the dialogue is so compelling is that it sounds as if they have just said it off the top of their head. It sounds real and genuine. Actors are paid dearly to make us believe something, and business professionals can take the cue. If you don't like feeling as if you are acting, than consider it "rehearsed spontaneity." The entire reason for you to practice is to gain confidence and come across in a compelling and professional manner. Here are some ideas:

- Say the message out loud a few times.
- If you stumble over a certain part, practice it over and over again.
- Start with the person's name, if possible. For example, if you are calling John because Bob recommended that you do so, start with, "John, Bob recommended that I give you a call."

- Call your own voicemail and record the message.
- Play it back. Is it a message the person will listen to?
- *Very important:* When you leave your phone number, picture the person on the other end of the phone looking for a piece of paper, then searching for a pen. If you give your phone number too fast, this will significantly decrease the odds of your call's being returned.

Content   Even if you leave a clear message with a phone number that the person can write down and a name that she or he can spell, if the message isn't compelling, it's doubtful that you'll get a call back. Here is a sample message to give you an idea of what you should say.

- If you were referred by someone, start there:
  - "Your attorney, Mr. Smith, suggested I contact you."
- If my attorney asked someone to contact me, I'd keep listening.
  - "He mentioned that you were looking for a web designer to help on a new project."
- You are immediately a problem solver—*not* just trying to sell your web designing services.
  - "I'd be very interested in talking with you about the project. [Pause!] My name is Susan Jones, and I can be reached in a few ways."
- You are now preparing the person to find a piece of paper and pen.
  - "I can be reached at 617-555-1212." Say each digit separately. It's not "twelve twelve," it's "one, two, one, two."
- Always leave your phone number. If it's not on the piece of paper the person is holding, the person doesn't have it!
- Make it easy for people to stay connected with you.

- "I'll also give you my email address if that would be a better way for us to connect. I can be reached at susanjones@ yahoo.com."
- If there is something that needs to be explained, such as spelling or punctuation, say so. If your name rhymes or sounds like something, use that as a way to be memorable and clear. For example, the people who sit near my office probably hear in their sleep, "Diane with one *n* and Darling like sweetheart."
- Your goal is to get a return call.
- Be personable and professional.

The message needs to provide enough specific information to let the person know what should happen next. For example, if you are reconfirming a meeting, say your name, the purpose of the call, the details of the meeting, and the way the person can contact you if there is a change, then thank them and give your contact info.

Here are some questions to ask yourself:

- Did you leave your contact information clearly at the beginning and end of the call?
- Is the receiver informed of what you do and why he or she should care?
- Does the receiver know what's expected of him or her? A phone call, an email, or something else?
- Does the receiver know what to expect from you?
- How would you rate your energy?

How to Get Your Calls Returned

When you are a sincere person with a valid question or idea, it's frustrating when you make a call, and your call isn't returned. You will increase your chances by following a few guidelines:

- Return all your calls. While others may not do so, really do your best and then try a little harder. Get the universe on your side.
- Make it clear what you are asking.
- Leave your phone number.
- Call during working hours. I find it unnerving when I get messages during off hours. Why not call me when I'm likely to be at my desk?
- Note: There are two reasons I don't return phone calls.
  - The person didn't leave a phone number, so I don't have it on the piece of paper where I wrote down the message.
  - I lost the piece of paper.
- Call again—you have three chances! Give the person the benefit of the doubt.

Summary: Well-structured voicemail messages provide a forum for the dialogue to continue. Use the technology to your benefit.

Your Outgoing Message

Here are some quick guidelines:

- If you don't like your voice, have someone else record the message.
- Script the message.
- Change your message if you are on vacation or won't be able to return calls within a day or so.
- Let frequent callers know how they can bypass the message.
- Include another way to get in touch with you.
- Say the number s-l-o-w-l-y and spell out any unusual words.
- Speak slowly so that people can hear what you say.

EMAIL

Email is a very useful tool that has revolutionized how we communicate. For some, it's the best invention since the wheel. For others, it's the collapse of civilization, grammar, and spelling. As with any form of communication, it is wise to take a few minutes and ask yourself if it is the best way to communicate your specific message. There is nothing right or wrong about email as a technology. How it is used is what matters. Take these items into consideration:

- As you sit down to compose a message, first ask yourself if email is the best method of communication for this message. Don't forfeit 93 percent of your communication power if you don't have to. If you are giving someone driving directions, email is ideal. If you are expressing yourself, you can be misunderstood fast.

- Make sure you know that it's a method the person you are trying to reach uses. If the answer is yes, then follow a few guidelines to ensure maximum impact.

- Think of your message as a postcard. The information can be interrupted, forwarded, or edited. Be sure that this is the best way to communicate. If the recipient chooses to forward it, how will that affect you and your business/career.

Your Name/Email Address

- Make sure that your email software is set up so that your name is visible to the receiver.

- People are looking at their inbox for your name, not your email address.

- If you are unsure of how to set this up, go to the Help section of your email program. For example, for Outlook, go to Inbox, then Tools, then click email accounts.

- Business email should use a professional email address. People may not remember that your email address is susan-jones@hotmail.com.

Subject Line

- Think of this as a headline. Imagine looking at a newspaper or magazine and skimming the headlines. That's what the other person should see when he or she sees the inbox. As the person is reviewing the "headlines," give her or him a reason to read your emails.
- In some cases you can actually communicate the entire message in the subject line (see Figure 12-1).
- If the entire conversation takes place in the subject line, the only reason to open the message would be to get the other person's contact information.

From	Subject	Received
George@yahoo.com	Meeting @ 3 p.m. confirmed	Mon. 10/2/2002 11:00 a.m.
Susan@aol.com	Can't do 2 p.m., 3 p.m. ok?	Mon. 10/2/2002 9:15 a.m.
George@aol.com	Reg mtg today @ 2 p.m.	Mon. 10/2/2002 9:00 a.m.

Figure 12-1 Email screen shot

CC

This should be used when everyone on the list knows everyone else and everyone has explicitly or implicitly given permission to have their email address broadcast, and when the email does not contain any confidential material. An example would be directions to a meeting or event, the agenda for a meeting, or event details.

BCC

- Always use this when an email is sent to a large group.
- Put your name and email address in the "to" line and all the other email addresses in the "BCC" line.

- Use BCC when those on the list would not want their email addresses shared publicly. For example, use it for a new email address announcement or new job information.
- When in doubt, use BCC.

Bullets

People read their email quickly. Consider using a bullet format, which provides an easy way for people to read the message. *Note*: This works only with HTML email, not text. With text, use hyphens instead.

!-Important

What you consider important, the recipient may not. Use the important flag (exclamation point) prudently.

Reply

Email is often sent back and forth. Typically other subjects get added in, and before you know it the subject is completely different. Change the subject line when the reply message is about a new topic.

Signature

- You wouldn't send out a letter without a signature, the same is true for email. At the bottom of each email should be a "signature." You may want to have several versions.
  - At a minimum, include your name and phone number.
  - Otherwise, add your title, the name of your company, your web site, your email address, contact information for your assistant, and all applicable phone numbers.
- If you don't know how to create a signature, click on the help section of your email service. It typically takes just a few steps, and once it's created, it automatically is included in each message.

Other

- Use proper grammar.
- Be aware that email can easily be intercepted.
- Know and follow the email policies at your office.
- Mis-sent email can have legal implications.
- Never send an angry email.
- Watch the clock. If you send business email at all hours of the night, you could signal that you are not a good time manager.
- If there is any possibility that your email could be misinterpreted, set up a phone appointment instead.

Summary: Using professional email techniques can facilitate and accelerate a business relationship.

SNAIL MAIL (A STAMP CAN MAKE THE DIFFERENCE)

Ask yourself how many emails you get a day. Now ask yourself how many handwritten thank-you notes you get.

We pay attention to handwritten notes because they are so rare. They get our attention. We save them at Effective Networking, Inc.

Put together a small envelope that includes note cards, stamps, and a pen. When you have finished a meeting (and certainly a job or information interview), sit in the lobby or your car and write a thank-you note. Put it in the mailbox. The satisfaction of completing the task is worth it. Be sure this is done within 24 hours.

Gents, this also applies to you! Get monogrammed note cards from a department store or a stationery store such as Crane's. I have received only a few handwritten business-related notes from men in my entire life, and I have them all. One got the sender mentioned in the dedication of this book.

The thank-you note is not your life story, the reason someone should hire you, or why your product is the best. It is simply to thank someone for his or her time and acknowledge that you appreciate his or her advice and ideas.

In all cases, include your business card in the thank-you note. Make it easy for the person to follow up with you.

Information interview thank you

Dear Mr. Jones,

Thank you for the time you spent with me, as well as your advice on transferring my skills and experience to the automobile industry. It's a very exciting field. I appreciate your willingness to have me get in touch with you after I have completed my MBA.

Thank you for your time.

Best, Joe Job Hunter

Sample thank-you after meeting at a networking event

Dear Sally,

It was a pleasure meeting you at the museum fundraiser. As promised, here is the article about sailing I mentioned. It was such a delight to meet someone who likes the sport as much as I do. I'm sure our paths will cross again.

Best, Mary Maven

Sample thank-you after first meeting with business prospect

Dear Jack,

It was a pleasure meeting you at the technical council event. I wish you luck in your entrepreneurial adventures. I look forward to our paths crossing in the future.

Many thanks—Robert Accountant

Summary: A first-class stamp sends the message that you are indeed a first-class person!

PERSONAL WEB SITES

A well-designed personal web site is affordable and is money well invested. You can build one for a few hundred dollars. This is a very worthwhile investment—in yourself and/or your business. Here are some guidelines to follow:

- Purchase your own name or something that you can use professionally.
- Build a web site. This doesn't have to be long—two or three pages is fine.
- Be professional (post any personal pages separately).
- Keep it current.
- Be sure that it can be printed without going off the page (portrait format).
- Have contact information on every page.
- Don't use your home phone number—have a separate line that children and other family members won't be answering
- Don't use your home address.

Summary: Best practices are just that—things that you practice as best you know how and on occasions push yourself to be better.

MAKE A CALL OR TAKE YOUR CALL—CRUCIAL DIFFERENCE!

The reason most people don't like to make calls is that they are afraid of rejection. Human beings naturally want success, and it is tedious to make calls and not get through. Thus, there is a crucial difference between making a call and having someone take your call.

You will significantly increase your chances of success if you set this up in advance as you are networking. Here are some ideas:

- Ask the person if it's okay for you to follow up.
- Find out the best way to do so, and suggest a phone call. You know the power of your voice; do what you can to maximize your chance of success.
- Ask if there are preferred times or days to call. Some people block off times where they don't take any calls.
- Inquire what is the name of his or her assistant.

Summary: There is a big difference between making a call and having someone take it. When you are networking, make a quality connection with the other person so that he or she will take *your call.*

HOW TO ASK FOR HELP! NETWORKING TO THE EXPONENTIAL POWER

You now know the importance of networking and making connections. Next, you need to ask people for help. Asking for help is hard for some people. They feel weak or needy. What's really happening is that we somehow think other people can read our mind and know what we need.

This became clear to me recently when I walked to the elevator in my apartment building. While I was waiting I put on my gloves, hat, boots, and all that extra garb you need during the winter. The elevator didn't come and I was getting frustrated. Then I realized what was wrong—I'd forgotten to hit the button. I laughed and realized this is how I often treat people. I expect them to help me—but I forgot to tell them what I need. In this case it was a simple ride down to the lobby.

During our networking workshops, we make time for people to introduce themselves and pose a specific question to the group. For example, if someone is looking to meet a particular person in a company, that person may ask if anyone can facilitate an introduction. We call this N_y^x.

Here are some of the examples:

- "I'd like to meet Mr. Jones at Top Drawer Computers. I'd like to explore a partnership. We offer strategic planning for medical device manufacturers."
- "We are seeking a new director of marketing. "If you know of any qualified candidates, please let me know."
- "Our neighborhood is seeking two to three people to help with planting a garden. If you know of someone who would like to participate, have him or her call 555-1212."

It's hard to ask for help. We don't want to appear needy. We don't want to "bother" people. The result? We confuse a need with being needy. Then we hint.

Lilly Tomlin is quoted as having said, "When I grow up, I want to be somebody. I guess I should have been more specific."

During this portion of the program for a group of women, someone said she had a question, but it was a bit off topic. "Go ahead and ask," I said.

"I really need a gold bag for a black tie on Saturday night."

The hands shot up!

Her request was specific, so many people were able to help her. People could visualize what a gold bag looks like, we knew her deadline, and many had been to a black-tie event.

- When preparing for a networking call or event, be sure you have an answer if someone asks, "How can I help you?"
- Be as specific as you possibly can.
- If you are a job hunter, don't say, "I'm looking for something in software." Say "I want to contribute my skills to a software company, such as Computer Associates, in QA helping to deliver quality products."

- *Note*: Depending on the forum, the term *QA* either will or will not make sense.
- Be careful about using buzzwords or slang that will intimidate others from helping.
- Give the listener a few options.
- Position yourself as a problem solver or a people developer.
- When networking to increase your practice or business, be sure you can say what industry is your target market, who is the decision maker, and, most important, what problems you can solve.

Summary: When you ask for help, say it in such a way that someone can visualize the situation. This will greatly increase your chances of success.

Before you head out to network, ask yourself, if someone offers help, what will you say? Answers such as winning the lottery are dreamy; however, they are not necessarily professional. Be specific; say "I've helped out several companies reduce their time from concept to delivery, particularly in the medical industry. Do you know someone at XYZ firm?"

When you grant people permission to say no, they appreciate it, and then the next time the two of you encounter one another, it's comfortable. You've been persistent, but you haven't stalked.

Summary: Know how to ask for help, know how to say thank you, and know how to give people the opportunity to say no.

A Lesson Learned

One of Boston's top executive recruiters, Deb Rosenbloom, uses this personal anecdote to illustrate a common networking mistake to avoid.

A number of years ago, I learned an important networking lesson the hard way. I was working in intelligence at the time, and I wanted to expand my career. Enthusiastically embracing the concept that "it's not whom you know, but whom you get to know," I set my sights on the Assistant Secretary of State for Politco-Military Affairs. I did all the right things to get an appointment. I found a mutual contact, used his name to send a letter, and requested 15 minutes for a purely informational conversation. Following up in a timely fashion, I got his assistant on the phone and made an appointment at the Pentagon. At the scheduled time and date, I showed up in my best polished, government look. I said all the right things to this powerful individual, quickly convincing him that I was a bright, high-energy, and competent young go-getter. Things were going smoothly until he asked, "So, Deb, how can I help?"

To this day, I cringe just thinking about the way I felt at that moment. I had executed my plan flawlessly. Here I was with the opportunity in hand, and I *had nothing to say*. In a split second, I went from competent go-getter to ineffectual time waster. I had requested an audience with a number two guy in the State Department, and I didn't know what I wanted from him.

Well, the pain and embarrassment have faded to a dull ache, but the lesson stuck. I never go into a meeting without a purpose, and I never ask for help unless the request is specific and actionable. And I try to pass on that lesson when I ask, "So, how can I help you?"

13

How to Maintain and
Grow Your Network

You want to keep your present network strong and healthy. When you maintain your network, you will never have to start from scratch again. Remember the effort that went into building it; now take care of it.

Here are some ideas:

- Once or twice a month, meet with someone you like—business or personal—and ask what you can do for him or her.
- Get involved with a professional association—get a leadership position or join a committee.
- Meet with your networking support groups (particularly your peer-to-peer team) on a regular basis—I suggest at least once a month.
- Write, speak, teach.
- Update your personal web site.

"When I Arrived in Boston, I Knew Two People"
~ Margaret Heffernan, former CEO of iCast

If there is anyone who understands the value of serendipity networking, it is Margaret. She likes meeting people. She is a bright and spirited Brit who moved to Boston when the economy in the UK was in bad shape. She recently returned and prior to her departure, we spoke about how she had managed to become so successful in Boston in a short time.

She started the conversation by saying that networking is how she got her first CEO job. Since she was new to town, the local headhunters didn't know her. The opportunity wouldn't have happened in a formal network — she would not have been included. And the person who recommended her wasn't a friend per se, but someone who knew enough to present her as a candidate.

Margaret has different interests and thus different networks. Some are colleagues, others are from her children's school or via one of her interests, such as music. When I asked whom she made time for in her busy schedule, she said the same thing that many others have: "It's important that I like them."

Here are some of her comments and insights:

- Be nice to people and help them.
- People give back in a number of ways—the currency is not always cash. It may be an introduction, referring business, or just being fun.
- Be fastidious about holiday cards.
- Keep a list of everyone you ever met.
- Networking is not linear.
- You can't be too deliberate.
- Connect yourself to networking nodes.
- Have genuine enthusiasm.
- Know how to have a good conversation.
- Networking is not an exchange of intellectual fluids.
- Networks need fresh fuel.

MAINTAIN YOUR NETWORK WITH PRESENT CLIENTS

In order to maximize your business contacts, you need to come up with a plan that will help you gain confidence when asking others to help you and also allow you to do some tracking of your present network. Here are some techniques.

Build your confidence with clients with whom you can speak candidly. Because you like them, and we'll assume they also like you, you are likely to get quality feedback. They will feel honored that you are taking the time to meet with them.

Here are some guidelines on why and how to network with present clients.

- You never know—the client may be ready to close on an account that will double its size, so that it will need more of your product or services.
- Build relationships before you need them. When a client relationship has gone sour isn't the time to invite the client to a special event in the community or a sports game.
- Consider bringing along someone else from the company who can help manage the relationship. This can be an excellent opportunity to invest in a rising star at the office by mentoring her or him. It's also a time when you can learn what is happening in the ranks that you may not be aware of.
- Ask the client for nothing except what you can do to help her or his business grow.
- Does the client have an open position and can't find the right candidate?
- Is the client less than satisfied with a service provider and seeking a new one?
- Is there a prospect that the client wants to close but can't seem to get a decision from?

- If one of the client's children has a new hobby, offer to connect the client to someone who can mentor the child.

- From what you've learned, come up with at least two or three things you can do that will make the client's life easier. In the course of a conversation, I once learned that someone was looking for a new team member. There were certain skill sets that the client wanted this person to have. A day or so before I had learned of someone who had done similar work, so I made an introduction that led to a job for one and a happy employee for the other.

- Introduce the client to a new supplier.

- Make a call on the client's behalf to a prospect.

- Invite the client to an industry event where she or he can get some visibility.

- Follow up within a week and provide an update.

- Each month put in a call to find out if there is anything new.

- The more you give, the more you get!

- Do the same for each of your other clients until the list is complete.

Remember, people are a bit like plants: They need to be watered, have good sunlight, and fresh air, and on occasion be repotted. Jeff Taylor, founder of Monster.com, said, "When you are unemployed is when you deploy your network—not when you create it." The same is true when you are making business development calls or requests for a nonprofit cause. Here are some thoughts:

- *Get started.* Be the one to get the relationship going. Take the initiative. Starting is often the hardest part. Make it easy for the other person. When the other person sees your energy and get-it-done attitude, she or he will share the information with others.

- *Create a system.* This can be index cards or a sophisticated software program. It doesn't matter—what does matter is that you use it.

- *When someone comes to mind, call him or her.* People like to know that they are thought of and, most important, that you took the time to connect.

- *Send thank-you notes.*

- *Send articles.* Don't assume that I've read an article that would be of interest to me. When you send an article, it reminds me that we share an interest. And as long as you don't stalk, you add a bit of currency to our business relationship.

In *The Tipping Point*, author Malcolm Gladwell states that it is our acquaintances that grow our networks.[22] It is when we reach beyond our present community that we grow and expand to new markets.

Bob Metcalfe founded 3Com Corporation and designed the Ethernet protocol for computer networks. Metcalfe's Law states, "The usefulness, or utility, of a network equals the square of the number of users."

In plain English, that means if two people have cell phones, that's nice for them, but the technology is useless for everyone else. The more people who have phones, the more valuable the network becomes.

When two computers are networked, they exchange information. The more computers that are networked, the more they can share. The same is true with people. Networking is an exchange. Get the wheels started and fuel the process.

> *I always do what I say I'm going to do.* ~ FIONA WILSON, PROFESSOR AT SIMMONS COLLEGE AND KNOWN IN BOSTON AS A "NETWORKING NODE"

PROFESSIONAL ASSOCIATIONS AND COMMUNITY ORGANIZATIONS

Professional associations are for people from the same industry or those who serve it. Community organizations are less targeted. It is crucial that you get involved with at least one organization at some point if you want your career to advance. This is where you can gain visibility within your industry with your peers, colleagues, competitors, vendors, and others. After you have attended several events, ask yourself

- Have I gotten any business from the organization?
- What role (if any) do I have?
- Would it be worthwhile to join a committee?
- Who from my firm is the keeper of the relationship with that organization?
- Is that person the right one for the job?
- What organizations should I consider joining in the next three to six months? Why? To further my career or get business for my company?
- Visit a new organization or meeting at least once a month.
- Determine the value of the group.
- Who should be the relationship manager?
- Create an action plan with next steps and a timetable.

PEOPLE WHO MAKE THINGS HAPPEN

Earlier in the book I spoke about the three different types of people —those who make it happen, watch it happen, or wonder, "what happened?" I also mentioned Benjamin Franklin and the "club for mutual improvement." I encourage you to be one of the people who makes it happen! Get active!

Participate in a few carefully selected clubs in such areas as investments, wine, books, sports, or other areas of interest to you. It's easy to focus too much on our business education; do something completely the opposite. Learn chess, a foreign language, or a new sport. In each of these communities, you will meet new people whom you can help and vice versa.

If you want to create a business-centric networking club, here are some things to consider:

- What is the membership duration?
- How often are meetings held?
- Where are they held?
- How are new members brought in?
- How are board members elected? Are there term limits?
- What is your mission statement?
- Invite business owners from different industries who are not competitors.
- How do you define a competitor? This is crucial, because sometimes we think someone is a competitor, and upon further review find that he or she is not. For example, someone who works at an auditing firm will surely encounter other CPAs in his or her career. In some cases, they may actually end up working together. They may serve different sectors or different size companies as well.

Invited to Join a Club?

> *"I refuse to join any club that would have me as a member."* ~ GROUCHO MARX

When you are invited to join any group, here are some things to consider:

- Who recommended the club?
- Are the fees and attendance requirements compatible with your lifestyle?
- Does the location lend itself to your attending?
- What are your goals, and does the club help you achieve them?
- Have you felt welcomed?
- Select only one or two groups to participate with in the beginning—give it at least six months.

ALUMNI GROUPS

We touched on this during the inventory exercise in Chapter 3. Now
that you know more, revisit this network and look for opportunities.

- Make a list of all the schools you have attended.
- Ask your executive team to do the same.
- Are there alumni groups in your area?
- Do they have regular meetings?
- When was the last time you attended one?
- Is there a visible role you can play within the organization?

VOLUNTEERING

Volunteering is one of the best ways to grow your network. Without
fail, almost every client I have I can trace back to someone I met
through some volunteer effort.

When you volunteer your time, you immediately put yourself
in a new category in people's eyes. You are more than just a business
professional, you are someone who cares about your community and
is willing to roll up your sleeves and do something extra to make a
contribution. Get active in a few strategic organizations.

There are a variety of deciding factors to consider:

- Does this group provide services by vertical market, or does
  it serve a special level of attendee?
- Are the people who attend decision makers, or do they influence the decision makers?
- Do I like the people I meet?
- What is my time and (other resources) commitment?
- Be sure you have time to honor your commitment; if you do not,
  it will come across that you were using the organization for your
  own personal gain and were not sincere about your offer.
- If you made a mistake, admit it, help find a replacement, and
  move on.

Summary: Only commit to things you really care about and you can carry out. It will hurt you in the long run if you say you'll take something on and you don't.

HOW TO HOLD INTERNAL NETWORKING MEETINGS

Many companies have an intranet. The purpose is to streamline internal communication, which is good. Take the time saved and host face-to-face internal networking sessions. Don't feel alone if your company hasn't done this yet. This is simple to do, is very cost- and time-effective, and builds morale. Here are some guidelines:

- The purpose is to provide a forum for people to share ideas, request a solution for a problem, and take a break from work.
- To start out, schedule the meetings once a month and put them on the calendar for the next three months.
- Continue on a monthly basis or consider holding them more frequently if the group would like it.
- Senior management must commit to attending and not canceling the session.
- Consider bringing in an outside facilitator.
- If you do not, find someone to facilitate who is in middle management—not at the top, but not too junior either.
- Test with a group of 50 or less.
- Serve soft drinks and snacks.
- The first 10 minutes should be for people to say hello to one another, get something to drink, and settle in.
- If the facilitator notices that people don't know one another, he or she can jump in and start making introductions happen.
- About 10 minutes into the event, the facilitator introduces him- or herself, welcomes everyone, and states the purpose of the session.
- Suggest that one or two senior management members say a word or two also welcoming the group and adding their

requests—"We're looking for a new vice president of engineering" or "My daughter has a school project on frogs, so if anyone is a frog expert, please let me know."

- Have some 3 × 5 cards and pens available on the tables, and let attendees know that they can pick up a card and write down their name and contact information and what they can do to solve the problem.

- Business requests can be as simple as, "I'm trying to figure out how to create a table in Microsoft Word." Or an account executive can ask if anyone knows someone at such and such company.

- The goal is to create a fun environment that is professional, but also conducive to information exchange within the company.

WRITING AND SPEAKING OPPORTUNITIES

Writing and speaking are two highly effective ways to increase your visibility—and therefore your network. You get instant credibility, for example, when a newspaper or magazine publishes your article. When you speak at a professional association, you get visibility and recognition from your peers that your competitors don't. Maximize these forums for your benefit.

Writing

Print publications always want quality content written by those in the industry. This is a great way to get your name and your company's name in front of numerous people in a cost-effective manner. When you write an article, you are considered an authority. It costs soft dollars—your time—rather than cash from an advertising budget. Some of the good things about an article are that it has a long shelf life and it can be shared with others. Here are some things to consider:

"Networkers Get Things Done"

Rick Daniels, president of the *Boston Globe* (owned by the New York Times Company)

During my conversation with Rick, we spoke at length about the value of building networks inside an organization. Often networking efforts are focused on people and companies on the outside. Those who learn how to master such relationships within their firms are seen by senior executives as more valuable and often receive promotions or recognition.

Here are some take-aways from our conversation:

- Become part of your community.
- Unless people know about you, it's tough to break in.
- Be a part of the knowledge system.
- Networking has its own velocity.
- It's a competitive advantage to have a strong network.
- It's not a numbers game—it's about quality.
- It makes future transactions easier.
- Know your Myers-Briggs preference.
- Anyone who is successful has mastered networking to a certain point.
- Take advertisers to lunch or to the Red Sox—you want to make them feel appreciated.
- Listen to fresh ideas.
- Nurture relationships inside and outside of your company.
- The best reason to get to know people in the organization is how much you can learn from them.

---

1. Select a publication that your clients read. You want them to see you in a new venue.

2. Writing is never finished. At some point, the deadline has arrived and the article is done; let it go! Don't be a perfectionist.

3. Frequency is preferable to length. Write often and write short, informative pieces.

4. Tell a story. Make it personal. It's easier to read and more memorable.

5. Don't pitch your product or company. Your article will never see the light of day if it's a puff piece.

6. Have a sense of humor. This makes an article much easier to read.

7. Work with a public relations agency.

8. Write letters to the editor.

Speaking

The best aspect of speaking is the interactive factor. There is a live exchange between you and the audience. This provides an opportunity for spontaneous banter. Because this aspect is not rehearsed, it is important for you to know your material and know it cold. This is not the best place to learn about your product or service and the nuances that differentiate you from your competitors. This is a preferred forum for more senior management team members who have credibility in their industry, are confident in their knowledge of the material, and have solid public speaking experience.

If you or someone in your company has this kind of opportunity or is a rising star, make the investment and hire a presentation coach. It will pay off. People will not always remember the person's name; however, they will remember the company's name. Your skills reflect not only on you, but also on your firm, industry, family, community, and more.

If you are invited to speak, here are some guidelines:

1. *Know the audience.* Weeks in advance, not the night before, find out who will be attending your presentation. If possible, find out the specific attendees so that you can read their bios.

2. *Prepare.* I find it totally insulting to hear a speaker say that the night before, he or she had no idea what he or she was going to say. (If that is the case, don't share it!) If the audience isn't that important to you, then don't agree to speak.

3. *Dress.* Your dress reflects your self-image. Be appropriate, and then up it a notch out of respect for the situation.

4. *Inform, don't sell.* You have been invited because you have knowledge that is considered valuable to the listeners. If you want to sell your product, then contact an ad agency. However, your positive impact and impression will help to sell your product or brand.

5. *Get the lay of the land.* Find the room where you will be presenting and check out all the equipment a few hours before.

6. *Share an example.* Telling an anecdote makes you human and accessible. It is also much more memorable than straight fact sharing.

7. *Avoid jargon.* If you use words that are unfamiliar to the audience, you will sound pretentious and lose your listeners.

8. *Contact information.* It's frustrating to an attendee not to know how to get in touch. Your coordinates should be on each page of your handouts.

9. *Cell phone.* Be sure your toys are turned off. It's quite embarrassing when the ringing phone turns out to be yours. Once I saw a speaker leave the lectern and rifle through his briefcase to turn off his phone.

10. *Use rehearsed spontaneity!* Practice! Practice! Practice! When you know your material and whom you are presenting to, you will be more relaxed and more interesting to listen to.

If the thought of speaking just terrifies you, take comfort. Public speaking is the number one fear—worse than death. With practice and help, you can overcome your worries and be a fine public speaker.

For years my neck would break out in a huge red splotchy rash. I had taken speech in high school and college; however, later in life I hit a wall of fright. Even in the summer I would wear turtlenecks that went as high as possible. Quickly I realized that this would be quite detrimental to my business, to put it mildly. I also realized that people liked the information they learned and that I was cheating them if I didn't share it. But my heart would race, my breath would become short, and I just wanted to be anywhere else. Overcoming the fear was no small task.

Two things helped: breathing exercises and proper preparation. When I feel flustered these days, I back my heels to the edge of the wall, stand straight, and take long, deep breaths. One time I was asked to participate in a discussion about networking with a sales team. We discussed expectations and the forum. When I arrived, things had changed, and instead of having an interactive discussion with a few people, I was suddenly expected to deliver a presentation for 20. I immediately felt my neck flame. I stepped out, got a tall glass of water, and did some deep breathing exercises. It helped immensely.

At the root of the angst is a normal fear of failure or embarrassment. We are human, we don't want to make a fool of ourselves. David Letterman said in an interview with Ted Koppel, "I have a very low threshold of embarrassment. I just don't like embarrassing myself. You know we have this—the theatre and the machinery and the people—and every day we try to put on a new show . . . and it all comes down to one hour, 5:30 to 6:30. If I somehow do something stupid that embarrasses me, I feel like I've thrown away that effort for the day. It's very frustrating . . . I think humans just don't want to embarrass themselves."[23]

Plenty of well-known performers, such as Barbra Streisand and Carole King, have experienced stage fright and thus imprisoned themselves in a recording studio. Through courage and friendship, they mustered the guts to take the stage again until they learned to conquer their fears.

We all want to be accepted and appreciated, and the thought of failure or humiliation is real. The truth is that practice improves our skills. If we practice avoidance, we will perfect our fear. By taking on the challenge and facing our worries, we put fear behind us and do not cheat others of our knowledge.

Start—just start. Begin speaking to small groups and run a few meetings—the more you do it, the less fearful you will be. Don't rob others of your knowledge. Do it for you!

> *I cannot give you the formula for success, but I can give*
> *you the formula for failure—try to please everybody.*
> ~ HERBERT BAYARD SWOPE

JOINING BOARDS

> *The act of self-giving is a personal power-releasing*
> *factor.* ~ NORMAN VINCENT PEALE

Serving on a board, either corporate or nonprofit, is an excellent way to make connections with people you otherwise would not meet. For those who are unfamiliar with board duties, there may be a hesitancy to commit to a board, especially after debacles such as Enron or Tyco. There are typically two types of boards for most companies: the board of advisors and the board of directors. The former is responsible for advice; the latter is responsible for both advice and financial management of the organization.

Start with an advisory position. Get to know players in the community, and determine if the position suits you personally and professionally. Board responsibilities can take a lot of time, and it's important to review the net results of any business or company awareness that comes from your role.

Nonprofit boards offer a different opportunity and a good introduction to board management. Ask around, find an organization that is compatible with your values, and find a way to serve. Start with a short term—one year. Nonprofits will expect you to make a cash donation and to help with fundraising. Find out what is expected of you before you sign up.

CAUSE-RELATED NETWORKING

Whether you pick a cause for personal or business reasons, it will reflect on both. Ask yourself why this organization appeals to you and whether this is the best use of your time. If the purpose is to grow your business, will this interfere with your business development efforts or enhance them? Be sure the audience meets the same criteria you have for a new customer.

- About 76 percent of consumers report that they would be likely to switch to a brand associated with a good cause (Cone/Roper Report, 1997).
- About 90 percent of workers whose companies have a cause program feel proud of their companies' values (Cone/Roper Report, 1999).

Here are some examples of cause-related programs:

- McDonald's and Conservation International
- Timberland and City Year
- MBNA and Ducks Unlimited
- Johnson & Johnson and Save the Children

One of the fastest-growing ways for companies to create visibility to is participate in a cause-related marketing campaign. "Cause-related marketing [CRM] refers to a commercial activity in which companies and nonprofit organizations form alliances to market an image, product or service for mutual benefit,"[24] according to the Business for Social Responsibility Organization. Remarkably enough, CRM also stands for customer relationship management. The two are interrelated in terms of the way you manage and leverage the assets of both groups.

Gail Snowden and Amy Geogan at Bank Boston saw an opportunity. Small loans to women business owners had a strong repayment track record and were highly profitable. They came up with what they thought was a brilliant business idea: Target women entrepreneurs.

The two made their business case to the bank executives and suggested that the bank sponsor a new nonprofit targeting women entrepreneurs. The bank was unconvinced, so the two found $50,000 out of their operating budgets to be the charter sponsors of the Center for Women and Enterprise in Boston. Soon the female entrepreneur was one of the fastest-growing and attractive markets in banking, and Bank Boston was at the forefront.

During this process, Gail and Amy developed a strong network that gave them visibility in the Boston area and the growing entrepreneur network. They made contacts while serving on the board that they otherwise would not have made. As more companies looked for working and expansion capital, the phone and profits started ringing at Bank Boston. The program was so successful that the bank decided to support other organizations serving the women's business community.

Neither of these women was the top executive of the company. They had budgetary responsibility and saw this as a business opportunity. The program's success gave the bank visibility in the community as well as those championing it.

Here are some key things to remember:

- Take care of your business and personal reputation.
- Treat the organization as if it were a paying client. Be on time with reports and deliverables.
- Underpromise and over-deliver.

While strategic partnerships with nonprofits can be very beneficial, they can also take time and energy. It is important for you to conduct the same due diligence you would with a for-profit partner. Nonprofits are typically short on resources—both people and money. Be clear about what you are able to provide (and expect), as well as what you cannot do.

When I worked for a nonprofit, we created several partnerships. One was with a cruise line, and another was with a manufacturing company. The cruise partnership was to provide funds for research. Through my former travel network, I learned that the company had recently been fined for environmental violations. In addition, the grant money came from casino profits. Now the nonprofit was taking "dirty" money.

The manufacturing company made its product in the third world and used child labor. It abided by the laws of the local country, however, some of the staff at the nonprofit were less than convinced that this was a good idea. The company was looking to leverage the visibility of the nonprofit to enter a new market and show its product in action. Management team members for both organizations changed, and the new players didn't develop the same rapport.

Both deals worked for a while, but they didn't survive in the long run. There wasn't enough of a bond and commitment by both parties.

Before you invest your company dollars and energy, here are some questions to ask when considering a partnership:

- Are the mission and values of the two organizations aligned?
- Who is on each board?
- Is the nonprofit a 501(c)3? (This is important for tax reasons.)
- Have the management teams met?
- Has either organization done this type of partnership before?
- Who is the relationship manager from each side?
- What resources will be allocated to the partnership?

OTHER NETWORKING FORUMS

A network is made up of a group of people who share an interest. A unique bond exists. In order to participate and feel comfortable, everyone needs to speak the same language if you will. Here are some examples:

"Networking Is a Recurring Commitment"

Pam Alexander, president of Alexander & Ogilvy

In the discussion with Pam, she spoke frequently of the importance of being involved in your community and sharing your expertise. Her firm did pro bono work for professional associations that served her market, and those connections led to business opportunities because people had seen her be successful.

She had many useful insights, and here are a few:

- Ask how you can leverage our expertise to help others.
- Identify markets you want to serve and find someone to champion you.
- Get people aware of who you are and what you do.
- Start networking by getting on boards.
- Diversify your clientele.
- Sharing your expertise gets you credibility.
- Think like a journalist—do your research.
- Whether you are paid or not, deliver value.
- Quantify your time commitment to others.
- Get everyone in your company involved in and committed to networking.
- Your firm is being hired not just for technology, public relations, legal expertise, etc. It is being hired for business development opportunities as well.
- Host dinner parties once a quarter with about 50 people.
- Invite high-quality and high-profile people.
- Assemble a group that has similar interests.
- Email is very effective—it's easy to forward.
- Generously share your knowledge.

- George went to work one day and had no idea what people were talking about. Apparently he was the only one who had not seen *Seinfeld* the night before. In order to participate in the office conversations, he started watching the show. He intentionally changed his behavior in order to fit in.

- When you walk by an office building, there is a networking group right outside—the smokers. They understand one another's needs in a way that nonsmokers don't.

- HOG[25] is a community that is 650,000 strong. What do they have in common? They own Harley Davidson motorcycles— Harley Owners Group.

- A strong and successful community is the 12-step recovery model. There is an understanding of a life challenge that others may not understand or appreciate. These groups are designed to provide a forum for people to share their fears and aspirations. The mission is not to get business, but the currency exchanged is often much more valuable than money.

- In parent-to-be groups, everyone is filled with anticipation and great joy. At the same time, each person realizes that his or her life is about to change dramatically. This also applies to weight-loss groups.

- When a member of our family becomes ill, we often feel alone. Learning that someone else is experiencing the same pain can help ease the burden and emptiness. Online support groups have mushroomed in the past few years.

- Fraternities and sororities are other examples of networking forums. When you see someone in an airport with a sweatshirt with the name of your house, you immediately sense a connection. A conversation can be readily started.

Summary: There are many groups out there—find one where you can learn, contribute, and be successful.

14

Ethics

A lie has speed, but truth has endurance. ~ EDGAR J.
MOHN

*Always do right. This will gratify some people and aston-
ish the rest.* ~ MARK TWAIN

In recent times, business scandals have led to a renewed interest in
ethics. As with almost anything, there is a fine line, and sometimes
it isn't clear until it is crossed. Networking is no different. As I inter-
viewed various successful professionals, I heard stories of people mis-
representing whom they know, their accomplishments, even where
they received their education.

Notre Dame and Dartmouth found themselves in the embarrassing situation of having to dismiss a new hire even before the person started. The United States Olympic Committee learned that its
chair really didn't have a doctorate as she had stated on her résumé.[26]

Your reputation is your most valuable life asset, both professionally and personally. Take pride in what you do, give proper credit
to those who have been a part of your success, and always be hon-

est. You will never regret it. It's easy to imagine that the team at Enron would like to redo a number of the decisions they made that proved catastrophic for themselves and many others.

Being ethical isn't the property of one gender, race, culture, or any other defined group. It's a behavior choice. When you are networking, state the facts. Here are some ways to protect yourself:

- Use someone's name only when you have been given permission to do so.
- Preferably ask someone to do an e-intro and/or make a call introducing you.
- It's okay to say, "I met John Jones at a trade show last week and he mentioned your name. I doubt that he would remember me, since he certainly met a lot of people that day."
- When in doubt, underplay your connection to the other person.
- You do not want to lead the other person to believe you have been endorsed. If you are being endorsed or recommended, a letter or email of introduction is appropriate.

Here's what I say when I write an e-intro. Conservatively, I write several a day.

- Roberta and Michelle—this is an e-intro from Diane Darling. The two of you should meet, and here are my thoughts.
- Michelle works for a company that is looking to donate a marketing tool to a nonprofit.
- Roberta is the executive director of a nonprofit that would value your services.
- Here is the contact information for both. (Include emails and phone numbers.)
- Over to the two of you!
- If you have any questions, please don't hesitate to contact me.
- Best—Diane

When you access someone under false pretenses, in due time it will be discovered. Don't risk it.

Here are some good guidelines for workplace ethics from *Power Etiquette*:[27]

- Don't participate in gossip.
- Be courteous and respectful to superiors and subordinates.
- Be positive and pleasant.
- Accept constructive criticism.
- Maintain personal dignity.
- Make an effort to preserve the dignity of others.
- Keep confidences and maintain confidentiality.
- Show your concern for others.
- Give credit to those who deserve it.
- Be honest.
- Keep your word.
- Encourage and help others to do their best.
- Make practice and constructive suggestions for improvement.

On occasion, you may want to confide in someone that you are starting a business or job hunting. Be cautious about the situation you are putting this person in. Are you compromising his or her job or relationships at all?

Unless we tell people what our ethical boundaries are, we cannot assume that both people see the same situation through the same glasses. In fact, if you are increasingly feeling imposed upon, it is probable that your expectations are indeed different. At that point, you can either choose to say something or back away. It depends on the value of the relationship.

As you think about networking, here are some ethical guidelines to consider.

Making Calls

It's intimidating to call people we don't know, even if someone has given us an introduction. Sometimes people use a variety of techniques to get access to someone. In some cases it's genuine, however, there are times when it is less than honest.

1. Have permission before using someone's name. Imagine that he or she is witnessing the conversation with you.
2. Respect the limits of your relationship. Don't overstate how well you know someone. The world is very small (and becoming increasingly so).
3. Be thoughtful of someone's time. Keep the call on topic and to the point.
4. Thank the person for his or her time and ideas.
5. Write a thank-you note.

Business or Personal References

Frankly, I pay little attention to references. I assume that the ones I'm being given are happy clients or a content former employer. This is where networking is either your friend or your foe. Any business community or industry is just a small community, when you get right down to it. Ask around and get the story behind the story.

If you have people in your past who when asked will say less than flattering things about you, address it quickly. Be proactive. In many cases there were two different styles or perspectives, and it was best for both parties to move forward separately.

Résumés

Your résumé should be both complete and accurate. Find someone who specializes in writing them. It will be worth your effort, time, and investment. If you think it is expensive, consider the alternative.

Summary: If you have to ask yourself if something is right or wrong, you already have the answer. Your career spans your life, not just one or two jobs. Be sure your behavior reflects your values (and those of the people who love you).

15

What If I Don't Feel Like Networking?

Ask yourself why you don't want to go to an event, or why you don't want to make the call. What is the *real* reason you don't want to attend? In some cases, it's simply that you are tired and have been working extra hours. Or the location of the event is not that convenient to the office. The location and logistics of getting to a destination play an important role in your decision. That's fine.

Note: The word *event* could mean a conference, meeting, trade show, dinner party, cocktail reception, luncheon meeting—any type of interaction with others that will require your participation.

What you want to avoid is not attending an event because of other reasons, such as fear of talking to people, intimidation, or concern that you won't fit in.

Practice makes perfect. If you practice not attending, then you will continually not feel like going to networking events. This is where you may meet future clients, friends, vendors, or employees.

"People Skills Are Dead Easy!"

Nicholas Boothman, author of *How to Make People Like You in 90 Seconds or Less*

Within a nanosecond of being on the phone with Nick, you feel his energy and enthusiasm for life and what he does. (Yes, the English accent helps too!) He has taken the mystery of how we connect with people and why, and he has truly demystified it.

We had an extensive conversation about shyness. Like others, he says that we are not born shy; instead, we are born cautious or reserved. We get embarrassed or humiliated when we do something, so that experience teaches us not to do it anymore.

He also talked about how making people like us isn't about whether or not they actually do like us, it's about how we make them feel. Do they feel valued, heard, important, or understood? Do we make them feel stupid or smart?

Some of the pearls of wisdom he shared during our discussion include the following:

- Get in a good mood.
- Unfold your arms and smile.
- Make people feel good.
- How does the other person make you feel?
- Adapt easily.
- Everything in life is about business.
- Business is about taking good ideas to market.
- Learn the weaknesses in your strengths.
- You can say "smile," but it's easier to make them smile.
- Anyone can do this.

HOW TO PSYCH YOURSELF UP

Sometimes going is not optional—we must attend an event. When that is the case, it's all up to you (and your attitude) how the event will turn out.

Here are some ideas that may make it easier:

- Find a networking buddy to attend the function with you.
- Treat yourself to a cab rather than public transportation and arrive in a peaceful state of mind.
- Research the event's web site for 15 minutes and write out your neutral questions.
- Remember a positive experience you had once before when you didn't "feel" like going.
- Consider the experience a "practice" event.
- Try a new introduction or challenge yourself to walk up to a few people and introduce yourself even when you really don't want to.
- Find one or two jokes that you can confidently tell. Practice them on a total stranger.
- Wear something that makes you feel great.

In many cases, it isn't as bad as you expected. In fact, frequently within 10 to 20 minutes, you find yourself in a great conversation that you otherwise would not have experienced.

Most people I've met consider networking something that needs to be done, not something that they want to do. When the discussion goes a bit deeper, it turns out that because networking is considered an important skill, there is an expectation that we know what to do. In reality, we haven't taken any courses in it, so it's a trial by fire experience.

Since networking doesn't immediately provide something tangible, we tend to discount its value and thus avoid it. When we practice avoidance, we lose our networking know-how, and that leads to discomfort.

DON'T KNOW WHAT TO SAY

This is one of the most frequent comments I hear. We put so much pressure on ourselves to say something meaningful or memorable. We forget that we can start with, "Hello, how are you?"

Joe was an accomplished young law associate. He was starting out in his law career, and he didn't see himself as someone who could bring in business for his firm or make an impact on the bottom line. He happened to be in Boston and came in for one of our workshops. A few days later, he was at the garage dropping off his car to be repaired and was getting a cab back to his office. The person next to him suggested that they share a cab.

During the training session, we had discussed conversation openers. Not sure of what to say during the ride, he started the conversation by talking about the fun dogs in the park as the cab drove into the city. After a few exchanges, they began to talk about what they did. It turned out that she was the general counsel for a company that his firm had been trying to approach.

Summary: It's worth it to be friendly. You never know!

FEEL LIKE WE'RE BOTHERING PEOPLE

We're only bothering people if we don't know what we want or what we have to offer. In that case, we are not thinking about others; we just are thinking about ourselves. Shift the focus to the other person. Each day people ask for help. Sometimes it's small—what supplier do you use for your business cards? Sometimes it's big—we're looking for $10 million in venture capital to start a technology business.

Most people would like to help people, preferably with the least hassle to themselves. If they know what your product or service is, or that you are seeking a new job, they can help everyone involved.

WE DON'T WANT TO APPEAR NEEDY

Neither does the other person. This is a hopeless stand-off—someone has to speak first. When you have done your preparation and your analysis of why you are networking and with whom, then you will be genuine and sincere. You will know what you have to offer and what the other person may need.

Having a need is very different from being needy. A need can typically be solved quickly and with one action—the right hire, funding for the business, getting a new job. Being needy is an ongoing and often draining experience for both parties. Articulate your needs.

FEAR

Fear is that little darkroom where negatives are developed.
~ MICHAEL PRITCHARD

Walking into a room, especially one filled with strangers, can be absolutely terrifying. There is one simple solution to this problem: Blame our parents! When we were younger and headed out the door, they were the ones who said, "Don't talk to strangers!"

The situation obviously has changed. We are no longer kids. We are adults, yet we still have childlike fears.

Here is a new look at the word fear:

- F—false
- E—evidence
- A—appearing
- R—real

What real evidence do you have that you should be afraid of saying hello to someone at a business or social event? The answer is simple—there isn't any!

As an adult, you have gained wisdom. You know that this individual may solve a problem that you have, and vice versa. Smile, reach your hand out, and say hello. If it turns out that there isn't any reason for the two of you to continue the dialogue, wish each other well. Simply say, "It was very nice to meet you! Best of luck."

Watch children—they are fearless. We have had the childlike curiosity trained out of us. Get it back! Take a look around the room;

is there really a reason for you to be intimidated by someone else there? It's likely that you all have something in common or you wouldn't be in the same room.

A forced conversation can feel like a nightmare. The next time we find ourselves in such a situation, we begin to worry and feel anxious. This means one thing—we are human. We want to be appreciated by others, and if we are rejected, it doesn't feel good. Therefore we ask ourselves, why risk it?

Fear of embarrassment, humiliation, rejection, shame, and all those other emotions makes us decide not to do something. Most of us did something as a kid that people made fun of. We learned from that experience not to do it again. We wanted to be accepted by our peers, and we learned what rejection felt like.

That moment also taught us that maybe we shouldn't try things we don't know how to do. We then shy away from unknown conversations or events to protect our self-esteem.

When you see someone with his or her arms crossed, that person is literally protecting his or her heart. In many cases, during that conversation the person is fearful of being hurt. Past experiences have taught him or her that there is reason to be afraid.

Suzanne Bates is an award-winning news anchor who now teaches public speaking. We were on a panel together at a conference, and she asked one of the participants to tell her story. The woman came up to the front of the room, leaned against the table, and crossed her arms. As Suzanne asked her questions, the woman's posture began to shift. Her shoulders began to look less like her earrings. Next, she dropped her arms and put her hands on the table. Within a matter of seconds, Suzanne made this person feel cared for and important. The woman no longer felt she needed to protect her heart by guarding it with her arms.

I have a collection of quotes on fear. Here are just a few:

- If you're never scared or embarrassed or hurt, it means you never take any chances. —Julia Sorel

- Anything I've ever done that ultimately was worthwhile . . . initially scared me to death. —Betty Bender

- Do the thing you fear to do and keep on doing it. That is the quickest and surest way ever yet discovered to conquer fear. —Dale Carnegie

- Winners are those people who make a habit of doing the things losers are uncomfortable doing. —Ed Foreman

- Fear defeats more people than any other one thing in the world. —Ralph Waldo Emerson

- Fear of success can also be tied into the idea that success means someone else's loss. Some people are unconsciously guilty because they believe their victories are coming at the expense of another. —Joan C. Harvey

- Feel the fear and do it anyway. —Susan Jeffers

- A champion is afraid of losing. Everyone else is afraid of winning. —Billie Jean King

- Fear makes strangers of people who should be friends. —Shirley Maclaine

- Whenever we are afraid, it's because we don't know enough. If we understood enough, we would never be afraid. —Earl Nightingale

DEALING WITH NERVES

When fear does strike us — and we are all human, so it will — here are a few exercises that take away the edge and reduce the stress. These take less than two to three minutes and work wonders.[28]

Exercise 1—Tension

- In your car or desk chair, sit where you can stretch your legs straight forward.

- Close your eyes if possible.

- Tense up your arms, legs, and shoulders and hold for 10 seconds.
- Relax.
- Take a deep breath.
- Tense up again for 10 seconds.
- Turn your head to either side, pull it down gently, and stretch your neck.
- Tense again. This time, be sure you point your heels to the ground and then point your toes forward.
- Relax your muscles. You're done in less than a minute!

Exercise 2—Breathing

- This one works well any time you are feeling the slightest bit of stress or strain. You can do this in an elevator, while walking, in your car, and so on.
- Sit up straight or stand.
- Close your eyes if possible (not recommended while driving).
- Put your hands to your side.
- Take a deep breath in to the s-l-o-w count of 4.
- Hold for four seconds.
- S-l-o-w-l-y breathe out for four seconds.
- Do this three times.
- If you are in a networking meeting or on a call and feeling anxious, this can be done anytime. It's quiet and unnoticeable.

Summary: When we are feeling tense and stressed is often when we get nervous and rush our words. In some cases, we come across as lacking confidence. In other cases, we come across as angry. Why risk a negative response? Take a breath and slow down.

WILL WE FIT IN?

This is a genuine concern from a practical standpoint as well as from an emotional one. We don't want to go into an event where we are not welcome or feel uncomfortable. We also want to be sure it is the right audience for us. One of the best ways to get an answer as to whether the organization might be a match for you is to ask someone who is familiar with the person or the hosting organization. What was this person's perception of the person or the group? What type of person is part of his or her network?

You will feel more confident if you do some pre-event preparation. Invest 5 to 15 minutes to determine whether the event passes or fails the screen test. Next, you will want to dig a bit deeper and learn more. What is your contact's role in the organization, how long has she or he been involved, to what other groups does she or he belong, and so on.

At this point, you have done more preparation work than most attendees will have even thought of.

From all that you have learned, draft up several neutral questions you can ask anyone in the room. (See Chapter 7 for some samples.)

Practice the questions out loud. Do this two or three times. Like magic, you'll feel much better, and you'll sound that way as well.

I'M NOT SURE IT'S WORTH MY TIME AND EFFORT

Time is precious. We can't get it back, and therefore we need to invest it wisely. There isn't anything worse than finding yourself trapped at an event or in a conversation when you could be working or off enjoying yourself elsewhere. Many networking events take place before or after working hours, so it is even more important to evaluate them for their immediate and long-term value.

Preparation is the solution. Review the event "Whether Report" (Figure 4-3) and determine whether or not you should attend. Now you have your answer.

ARE YOU HESITANT TO DEPLOY YOUR NETWORK?

It's great that we have a collection of wonderful people that we can help. However, we often don't call on them when we need to. We trick ourselves into believing that if they could help us, they would have done so already. Or are they too busy? Do they even know what we need? I've seen this happen to the best of networkers. It's a subtle form of self-sabotage.

People don't want to feel that they "owe" you. The best way to keep the relationship going strong is to ask them for their advice or help in something. They will feel honored that you—a champion networker —asked them. Many of us are perfectly willing to call on our business network, but it's harder to call on our personal one. Don't interrupt the networking process. If you don't ask for help, others will be hesitant to ask when they need help. This a full-circle effort. It's time to punt!

Begin by asking for little things. Request something that is easy for the person to say yes or no to. For example, if you ask to borrow someone's jacket to run an errand when it's cold outside, the person is likely to say yes. Of course, the person may say no because he or she is also heading out in a few minutes and will need it. This isn't a rejection of you; it's a turn-down of that specific request.

In *Men Are from Mars, Women Are from Venus*, John Gray explains why men don't like the word can. Can you take out the trash? Of course, they can—whether they will is a different question. Learn how people like to be asked to help you. It's as simple as do they speak French, German, Spanish, or English. You need to ask in the right language.

Hinting   While we may think our friends or business associates are brilliant, they really can't read our minds. Don't make it difficult. Come straight out and ask them if they know someone who would help with such and such a project. In many cases they are waiting for permission to help. They may have offered in the past and someone didn't like it. So they are concerned about offending you. Teach them that you are different and that you would very much like their assistance.

Genuinely Flatter Them　"Of all the people I could ask, I knew you would have the answer."

Remember the story of the person in Texas who asked for the gold bag, black tie, Saturday night. Make it memorable, repeatable, and simple.

I'M NOT THE NETWORKING TYPE—I'M SHY!

Most people think that good networkers are sociable types—outgoing, eager, people who can walk up to anyone with ease. Some of those people are indeed excellent networkers, but not necessarily.

Shy people can be excellent networkers. It's not about walking into a room and slapping people on the back. Networking is about being genuine and sincerely interested in others. Quiet and introverted people can be very genuine and sincere. In fact, many would argue that it is the quieter people who fly under the radar who know what's really happening and who are the players.

Susan is someone I've known for nearly 10 years. We met at a slide show that a friend was giving, a book signing about his brother, who decided to work in the circus as a clown. Needless to say, there were a variety of conversation topics at this gathering. In the years I've known Susan, I've observed that her ability to stay connected with people, sincerely care about them, make introductions, and much more, is truly an art.

Curiosity and genuine interest—these characteristics are essential to networking success.

As I researched this book, I became fascinated by the impact of shyness on people's lives. The research also helped me understand myself. While I am touted as a superb networker, that doesn't mean that I don't feel nervous when I walk up to strangers and start a conversation. Like flossing, I'm very competent at it. But I would always prefer someone to introduce him- or herself to me rather than my making the effort.

When I surveyed a group of senior executives prior to an event, over 60 percent said that they were either somewhat shy or very shy.

Shyness is rooted in a range of legitimate fears, namely, fear of

- Failure
- Embarrassment
- Rejection
- Humiliation
- Shame

We remember those times when we were children and someone made fun of us. If we were not in an environment where we could repeat the behavior and get a positive rather than a negative response, we assumed that we had done something wrong or bad. The next time we were in a situation where we could try the behavior again, we opted to avoid the potential embarrassment and not participate. We practiced avoidness and therefore perfected it.

As we contemplate attending an event, we can find ourselves experiencing "anticipatory anxiety." We begin to experience nervousness just thinking about it.

Vijai P. Sharma, author of *People-Fear, A Self-Help Book for Social Anxiety and Social Phobia*, says, "Social anxiety refers to the nervousness we feel when we are around people. 'Stage fright' is the nervousness or fear a performer experiences about his or her public appearance. But what is a 'stage' anyhow?"

All the world's a stage,
And all the men and women merely players.
They have their exits and their entrances;
And one man in his time plays many parts.
~ Shakespeare, *As You Like It*

Nine out of ten people have stage fright.[29] For some, just introducing themselves makes them feel as if they are on stage.

Dr. Sharma reminds us of Bashful in *Snow White*, the shy and nervous character named Piglet in *Winnie-the-Pooh*, and the Lion in *The Wizard of Oz*, who is "afraid of everything and everybody."[30]

When we were children, these stories were used as a part of our character education. The Lion believes that the Wizard has the power to give him courage, only to realize that he had it all along.

"Toxic Sensitivity to Emotions"

Jonathan Berent, author of *Beyond Shyness*

It is frequently said that fear of public speaking is the number one phobia in society. What is often not said is that for someone who thinks of him- or herself as shy, public speaking is talking to anyone — not just making a speech or a presentation. Even just saying hello can be extremely painful.

In the conversation with Mr. Berent, he said that there are two types of people who consider themselves shy: Those who are so terrified that they don't leave their home, and those who are "highly functional," such as executives who are so intimidated at the thought of taking a client to lunch that it is affecting their career.

We spoke several times, and what stayed with me the most was the choice that someone makes about her or his behavior. Whatever people repeat, they reinforce. If someone doesn't go out of her or his comfort zone and talk to strangers, then the fear will continue and in some cases increase.

Most of these people are treatable and in fact lead very successful lives. Advertising has tricked many into self-diagnosis and thinking that a pill is the solution, when for most some behavior modification is the key to long-term healing. The process of healing includes the difference between performance and identity. In other words, just because someone does something that people laugh at doesn't make her or him a bad person.

In our conversations, he repeated what others had said: Shyness is learned. It is often the result of ongoing teasing and/or repeated embarrassment that went unresolved. For many this is a traumatic situation, and when it has been buried for years, it steals the childlike expressiveness that people wish to have.

Here is some of his advice for you or someone you know who suffers from shyness:

- Get out of your comfort zone.
- Learn to understand your fears at a deeper level.
- Don't be addicted to avoidance.
- About 50 percent of his clients have a learning disability—get tested.
- Shy people are more susceptible to mistakes, failure, and low self-esteem.
- People can change very quickly, depending on how motivated they are.
- Mental hurts can turn into physical pains, and you can experience a panic reaction.
- Get help from someone you trust.

Essentially, what I learned from my conversations with him and others about shyness is that because we have learned the behavior, we actually need to unlearn it and then retrain ourselves. This can take time; however, it is worth it.

INNER CRITIC

Not only do we have many external messages about why we should be less than thrilled to venture out, we have internal messages as well. We hear over and over again in our minds that we should be hesitant to venture out. We hear all the reasons why we might fail. We may not fit into the group. Others know more about what they are doing than we do. Our clothes aren't right. Even our hair affects our state of mind.

With all that negativity, no wonder we are less than excited about venturing into the unknown. The truth is, we have mixed feelings. We want to attend so that we can make a contribution, share our knowledge, and help others. We also want to be accepted and appreciated. On the other hand, we could experience negative emotions—we may not be welcomed, we will feel alone if we don't find someone to talk to—and this translates to our feeling rejected.

We all have an inner critic. Networking is a perfect time to convert that voice to a positive one. Instead of saying

- I don't want to go. I won't meet anyone whom I can do business with. Plus, I'd rather be home watching TV.
- The last time I went to one of these things, I just met competitors.
- I don't like small talk and I never will.

Replace it with

- I'll give it 15 minutes. If I don't feel inspired by then, I'll give myself permission to leave.
- Competitors can be interesting to talk to. It's interesting to learn what is going on in my field.
- I'm going to write out three questions I can ask anyone in the room and test them to see which one works best.

DEFINITION OF INSANITY

Many of you are familiar with the definition of insanity: Doing the same thing over and over again, but expecting different results. If networking is truly working for you now, change nothing. If you keep doing the same thing over and over again, but expect a different result, maybe you should rethink your efforts.

16

Gender, Race, Culture, and Other Networking Factors

Stereotypes abound. It's a fact. No matter how much we don't want to admit it, when we meet someone, we immediately bring with us a flood of stereotypes as to how that person should behave. Gender, race, culture, religion, age, political affiliation—whatever group we are a part of, either by birth or by choice, others have pre-conceived expectations of how we will behave and will approach us with that in mind. Movies and books either celebrate the differences or try to explain them.

GENDER

The two main categories we are lumped into are male and female. This starts at birth and goes on for life. The moment we walk in the door, there are assumptions made about us. This inescapably affects networking—where we network, the time we have available, and what is expected and/or permitted.

The increasing number of organizations dedicated to women in business indicates that they have not felt welcomed by men and feel a need to self-segregate.

THE OLD BOYS NETWORK

One of the most talked about networks is the "old boys network." Men have been networking for a longer time than women. It's just a fact of the business world. They have had more practice and experience at it. However, that is changing as more women are in the business world and have been for a while.

The "old boys network" exists. It is important for women to meet and work with men who are "in the know" and who want to facilitate introductions for talented women in the business community. Women who speak their business language and help facilitate the growth of companies will find it easier to break into the old boys network.

In June 2002 Anita Hill wrote an article for the *New York Times*[31] pointing out that the whistleblowers at Enron and the FBI were both women. *Time* chose them as Persons of the Year. Are women more ethical, or are they left out of the "old boys network" and therefore feel more free to speak out? It's an interesting question, and one that doesn't have an easy answer. The bottom line of business is profit. If you can help a company grow profits—ethically— you will be in a network of talented people of both genders.

RACE, CULTURE, WEIGHT, AND OTHER NETWORKING FACTORS

The same is true with race and culture. Increasingly I'm invited to speak for groups such as the Latino Professional Network. There is a self-selective segregation going on so that people can reach out to like-minded others to learn, network, and do business. These organizations are growing in size and power as their members are reaching higher roles in companies. Companies such as Gillette and Verizon have diversity initiatives so that the company's employee base reflects its customer base.

As a child and a teen, I lived in Asia. We didn't have a TV, and neither email nor the web were used by the public. Being a racial minority was something I learned about early. There were traits I learned to attribute to the Thai population. Some of them were refreshing and infectious, as Thailand is indeed the "Land of Smiles."

When our family returned to the United States, we moved to Alabama. One of my most indelible memories is of the time our family went to Tuskegee Institute for the Christmas concert. There were *maybe* 10 Caucasians in the entire concert hall. As I watched the various groups head to the stage, I marveled at the casualness of the performance and the performers. There were outbursts of laughter, spontaneous applause, and audience participation. That certainly wasn't how I had been taught to behave at a religious or holiday event.

Whether they are based on race, gender, religion, or culture, we all make judgments throughout the day. Some of the popular TV shows, such as *Mork and Mindy* or *Third Rock*, make us realize how ridiculous those assumptions are. But they are real, and it is wise for us to accept this and learn the best way to manage the situation, no matter where we are.

The film *Shallow Hal*, starring Gwyneth Paltrow, addressed the topic of weight and how we think about it.[32] Ms. Paltrow was startled at how she was treated when she was in New York wearing her "fat suit." She said, "I walked through the lobby. . . . No one would make eye contact with me because I was obese. The clothes they make for women that are overweight are horrible. I felt humiliated because people were so dismissive."

We make instant decisions about people based on these and other factors. There is nothing we can do to change this. However, smart networkers are aware of it and how it can positively or negatively affect others as well as themselves.

THREE MOST IMPORTANT NETWORKS

While it is tempting to be influenced by the networking factors discussed previously, at the end of the day we fall into three networks:

- SM—Smart
- NS—Not Smart
- S—Stupid

It's smart to network with others whom you can help and vice versa. It's not smart to have race, culture, gender, or *anything* other than genuine talent affect your decision. It's downright stupid to make a decision based on any of those factors before you meet someone.

If you discover that you are networking and not being successful, ask yourself if you are in a community of people who genuinely appreciate you for what you offer. Some are better than others.

Summary: Life is too short—don't waste your talents on people and communities that don't appreciate them.

17

Evil Networks

I would be remiss if I didn't discuss one of the most famous networks that, sadly, the world now knows—the Osama bin Laden network. This group decided to pull together its resources and energy and use them in a destructive manner. Not all networks put their genius to good use. A friend from college had to extricate his daughter from a cult that had infiltrated her college dorm.

Any time we are asked to think or do something that we feel is wrong, it is time to evaluate the network and consider leaving. Do not stay in an environment where you are asked to compromise your values.

18

Summary

My first car was a VW bug—with optional heat. And those were the days before fleece. I had a bulky sleeping bag in the car that I would wrap around me so that I could have my shoulders covered and my feet out for the pedals. As I learned to master the clutch, I also discovered a muscle on the backside of my left leg that for the previous 20 years had gone completely undetected.

However, nothing was going to stop me from learning how to drive my new-to-me $800 magical machine.

Most of us clearly remember our nervous state of mind when we first learned to drive. Add to that the complications of a stick shift. Juggling our eagerness for freedom, the driving instructor's nerves, a few plastic cones, and a large parking lot, we were all set!

Clutch in, slowly pressing the accelerator—cough, cough!

What happened? We stalled.

As unbelievable as it may be, we didn't get it right the first time. Even now, when some impatient person is behind us in traffic, beeping to tell us how much he or she wants to be our new best friend, we rush, pop the car into gear, let out the clutch, and stall.

In due time, the percentage of successes far outpaced the stalls. We were on our way to a new and exciting sense of freedom. Our new-found skill gave us confidence and a sense of adventure to explore the unknown.

Networking is similar. We need to be patient with ourselves. We didn't master all the moving parts of letting out the clutch, pressing the accelerator, and shifting the gears the very first time we tried it. The same was true with our first step.

Why do we expect to be proficient at networking? Unlike the situation with driving, where there are driver's education classes and state exams, we haven't had any training or education in networking.

Now let me ask you which is more important, the car or the gasoline. If you had to pick either hardware or software, what would you choose?

The questions are pointless. Why would you want a car without gasoline? Likewise if you had great software, but no computer to use it with, what's the point?

The same is true with "hard skills" and "soft skills."

Rarely is a business or person selected simply on the basis of business or technical skills. Sovereign Bancorp chief executive Jay Sidhu told a audience of analysts that 90 to 95 percent of a person's success depends on "emotional intelligence." He went on to say that "we assume our leaders have some IQ. You also need human skills to be a great leader."[33]

When I got the call to write this book, I calmly said, "Sure, no problem." Then I woke up and stared at the ceiling—what have I done? Next, I was on the phone calling people I knew and saying, "Would you be able to talk to me for a few minutes about a project?" Then I started meeting all kinds of new and fascinating people. Now close this book and make a call. Just say hello and ask what you can do for the person.

Happy networking!

Resource Guide: Products, Services, and Tools to Make Networking Easier

There are many products and services I use to help make my life easier. Some are obviously related to networking, such as PDAs or cell phones. Others make me feel more confident, such as clothing, briefcases, or even breath mints.

The following is a list of some of these products and services. If there is one you think we should know about, send an email to: Info@EffectiveNetworking.com.

Product or Service	Web	Comments
Newspapers and Magazines		
Zinio	www.Zinio.com	Online service that lets you download publications such as PC Magazine and flip through the pages as if it was paper. Reduces weight in your briefcase. Limited number of magazines available, but that will improve with time.
The Wall Street Journal	www.WSJ.com	The ultimate in news. A must read for everyone.
The New York Times	www.NYTimes.com	Get the Sunday issue if you are outside of New York.
The Christian Science Monitor	www.CSMonitor.com	An excellent, well-written paper with a wide variety. of articles.
Business Journal	www.BizJournals.com	Subscribe to your local city version. Excellent information and articles.
Time or Newsweek	www.Time.com or www.Newsweek.com	It's worth subscribing to one of the news weekly magazines.
BusinessWeek	www.BusinessWeek.com	A must for those in the business community and those that service it.
Fortune	www.Fortune.com	Thoughtful stories about business today.
Fast Company	www.FastCompany.com	Unique perspective on business—especially the people aspect.
People	www.People.com	While there's a lot of celebrity stories, there are also ones of "real" people. Sometimes I just enjoy reading the magazine when I'm at airports and want light reading.
USA Today	www.USAToday.com	Great reading especially when you are on the road.

Product or Service	Web	Comments
Hardware Tools—Computers, PDAs		
Dell	www.Dell.com	Excellent quality and service. A bit confusing to order— too many choices and can't touch the computer before you buy.
IBM	www.IBM.com	Solid machines—a bit heavier. Now have both the touchpad and button.
Toshiba	www.Toshiba.com	Machines are getting lighter. Button mouse.
Tablet PC	www.TabletPC.com	This is a new product and one of the few on the list I haven't actually used. However, my sense is it will be a very good product for those who like to write notes and have a PC with them.
CardScan	www.CardScan.com	Scans business cards into your database—Outlook, ACT, Excel.
Treo	www.Handspring.com	Combination cell phone and PDA. This one is more of a PDA first.
Kyocera	www.Kyocera.com	Combination cell phone and PDA. This one is a phone first. I have the B&W version which I adore. I understand a color one is coming out soon.
TiVo	www.TiVo.com	Record shows that you can watch whenever you want. Great way to catch news magazines or something light such as Leno or Letterman.

(continued)

225

Product or Service	Web	Comments
Software Tools		
Trillian	www.CeruleanStudios.com	Use multiple instant messaging services with just one application. Note: if you type in the web site trillian.com, you will get something a bit more extraterrestrial.
Egrabber	www.eGrabber.com	Lets you highlight text on emails or web sites and transfer the data to your database without retyping.
ACT	www.ACT.com	Database software that can be customized.
Roving	www.Roving.com	Email marketing tool.
Quicken	www.Quicken.com	Helps you track your expenses, such as networking events, and relate them back to customers.
Inspiration	www.Inspiration.com	A fun, useful tool to inventory your networks, brainstorm, and much more.
Writing Tools		
Dictionary	www.MerriamWebster.com www.Dictionary.com	Great sites to help you choose the right word
Bose Headphones	www.Bose.com	These headphones are just phenomenal. My office is located in an open space and can be quite noisy. These are also great for those who fly.

226

Product or Service	Web	Comments
Shoes		
Rockport	www.Rockport.com	It's essential to be comfortable especially when you are at a trade show or conference. Both Rockport and Timberland fit the bill. Styles are improving, especially for women.
Timberland	www.Timberland.com	Comfortable and the styles are improving, especially for women.
Good Feet	www.GoodFeet.com	Insoles made so you can wear your own shoes more comfortably.
Clothing		
Brooks Brothers	www.BrooksBrothers.com	Affordable, classic clothes for both men and women. Excellent service.
Barry Bricken	www.BarryBricken.com	Classic clothing for both men and women.
Armani	www.Armani.com	Fashionable and well made.
Joseph Abboud		Sharp, attractive clothes for men who like style and comfort.
Talbots	www.Talbots.com	Tailored clothing for women. Catalog or stores.
Nordstrom	www.Nordstrom.com	Top customer service.
Saks Fifth Avenue	www.Saks.com	Good variety. Consider working with the personal shopper.

(continued)

Product or Service	Web	Comments
Briefcases and Business Card Cases		
Levenger	www.Levenger.com	Catalog company with top-quality products for business professionals.
Coach	www.Coach.com	Classic briefcases and leather products.
VistaPrint	www.VistaPrint.com	Excellent quality, inexpensive business cards. You only pay postage.
Oral Hygiene		
Listerine Pocket Paks	www.PocketPaks.com	Flat, strong, melt-on-your-tongue mints. They are quiet and discreet and work very well.
Altoids	www.Altoids.com	A favorite of many.
Breath Alert	www.Tanita.com	This small device lets you know if you have bad breath.
Mentos	www.Mentos.com	Soft mints for those who like to have something to chew.
Peppermint Patties	www.Hersheys.com	A wonderful combination of chocolate and mint. Best in cooler climates.
Brite Smile	www.BriteSmile.com	Teeth whitener for those who like the service provided.
Crest	www.Crest.com	Teeth whitener for those who like to do it themselves at home.
Dental floss, brush	www.OralB.com	An excellent variety of products to help you keep your teeth clean and healthy.

Product or Service	Web	Comments
Personal Care		
Cleaning wipes	www.Lever2000.com	Great for hot days or those who have sweaty hands.
Hand sanitzer	www.Purell.com	A must when at a trade show or conference.
Lipstick	www.Lipsense.com	The only product that really stays on. It even comes with remover.
Mascara	www.Lancome.com	Stays on and doesn't smudge.
Lauren Hutton	www.LaurenHutton.com	She's created a makeup line for those of us with "mature" skin. And she's not robbing us in the process.
Shyness Web Sites		
Shyness Institute	www.Shyness.com www.Social-Anxiety.com www.Social-Anxiety-Network.com	Has a quiz to determine your level of shyness. It's a bit confusing, but asks some good questions.
Boston University Anxiety Clinic	www.bu.edu/anxiety /adult.html	Largest type of a clinic in the United States. Extensive treatment options for those with various social phobias.
Business Web Sites		
OnBusiness Network	www.OnBusiness Network.com	This is an excellent site created by Cisco dedicated to business education.

(continued)

Product or Service	Web	Comments
Google	www.Google.com	Search engine. Install the tool bar as it lets you highlight the words you are searching for on the pages found.
Copernic	www.Copernic.com	This is an application you download and it searches several search engines at the same time.
Amazon	www.Amazon.com	I frequently buy used books here as well as new.
Chase	www.Chaseonline. Chase.com	Their tag line is "The right relationship is everything" and they have it nailed. The best part about Chase One Place is that everything is literally in one place—bank accounts, investment accounts, even frequent flyer programs. It gives you a one screen.

Professional Association Web Sites

Product or Service	Web	Comments
Meeting Planners Int'l.	www.MPIweb.org	This site will help you find a meeting planner.
Int'l. Special Event Society	www.ISES.com	They are dedicated to special events.
Image consultants	www.AICI.org	Association for image consultants. Has a directory to help you find someone.
Professional organizers	www.NAPO.net	If you would like to find a professional organizer who can help you create a plan to organize your space and time, contact one of these people. It's a very worthwhile investment. Note: the .org will take you to a police organization.

Notes

[1] Autobiography of Benjamin Franklin, online. http://eserver.org/books/Franklin

[2] History of Rotary. RotaryHistory.org

[3] www.first15seconds.com

[4] http://livingheritage.org/three_princes.htm, The Three Princes of Serendip by Richard Boyle, 2000.

[5] Merriam-Webster

[6] The Forum Corporation research quoted by Tom Peters

[7] Nick Cafardo, "First Impressions," *Boston Globe*, August 17, 2002, p. E1.

[8] Press release on Yale study.

[9] Sheryl Lindsell-Roberts, *Business Writing for Dummies* (Foster City, CA: IDG Books Worldwide, Inc., 1999).

[10] Richard C. Whiteley, Love the Work You're With (New York: Henry Holt, 2001), p. 157.

[11] Nicholas Boothman, *How to Make People Like You in 90 Seconds or Less* (New York: Workman Publishing 2000), p. 55.

[12] Beauty Before Age, San Francisco and Mill Valley. www.beautybefore-age.com.

[13] Dotty LeMieux, "Here's the Wrinkle on Botox," *San Francisco Chronicle*, May 3, 2002.

[14] http://www.epromos.com/EducationCenter/messsendbooth.jhtml.

[15] Networking Survival Kit is a trademark of Effective Networking, Inc.

[16] http://www.apa/org/journals/psp/psp791110.html.

[17] http://www.fortune.com/indexw.jhtml?channel=artcol.jhtml&doc_id=209509.

[18]From Todd Bidwell, Cooper Productions, www.cooperproductions.com.

[19]www.robertsrules.com.

[20]Press release from Nancy Michaels, Impression Impact.

[21]Dana May Casperson, *Power Etiquette: What You Don't Know Can Kill Your Career* (New York: AMACOM, 1999).

[22]Malcolm Gladwell, *The Tipping Point*, (New York: Back Bay Books, Little, Brown and Co., 2002).

[23]Ted Koppel interview with David Letterman, July 9, 2002. For transcript go to: abcnews.go.com/sections/UpClose/DailyNews/upclose_letterman_transcript_020708.html.

[24]www.BSR.org—Businesses for Social Responsibility.

[25]www.hog.org—Harley Owners Group.

[26]Jeffrey Kluger. "Pumping Up Your Past," *Time*, June 10, 2002.

[27]*Power Etiquette*, p. 121.

[28]Learned exercises from Dr. Alison Domar, Harvard Mind Body Institute.

[29]Vijai P. Sharma. *People-Fear, A Self-Help Book for Social Anxiety and Social Phobia*. Mind Publications, p. 12.

[30]Ibid, p. 9.

[31]Anita Hill, "Insider Women with Outsider Values," *New York Times*, June 6, 2002.

[32]http://movies.go.com/news/2001/8/gwynethfatsuit082101.html.

[33]Scott Bernard Nelson, "A Scientific Detailing of Warm, Fuzzy Leadership," *Boston Globe*, April 14, 2002.

Bibliography

Berent, Jonathan, and Amy Lemly. *Beyond Shyness: How to Conquer Social Anxieties.* New York: Simon & Schuster, 1993.

Bolles, Richard Nelson. *What Color Is Your Parachute? A Practical Manual for Job-Hunters and Career-Changers.* Berkeley, Calif.: Ten Speed Press, 1970.

Boothman, Nicholas. *How to Make People Like You in 90 Seconds or Less.* New York: Workman Publishing, 2000.

Brooks, Donna, and Lynn Brooks. *Seven Secrets of Successful Women.* New York: McGraw-Hill, 1997.

Carnegie, Dale. *How to Win Friends and Influence People.* New York: Pocket Books, 1981.

Casperson, Dana May. *Power Etiquette: What You Don't Know Can Kill Your Career.* New York: AMACOM, 1999.

Covey, Stephen R. *The 7 Habits of Highly Effective People.* New York: Simon & Schuster, 1989.

Fox, Jeffrey J. *How to Become a Great Boss.* New York: Hyperion, 2002.

———. *How to Become a Rainmaker.* New York: Hyperion, 2000.

———. *How to Become CEO.* New York: Hyperion, 1998.

Gladwell, Malcolm. *The Tipping Point: How Little Things Can Make a Big Difference.* Boston: Little, Brown, 2002.

Goss, Tracy. *The Last Word on Power.* New York: Doubleday, 1996.

Gottesman, Deb, and Buzz Mauro. *The Interview Rehearsal Book: 7 Steps to Job-Winning Interviews Using Acting Skills You Never Knew You Had.* New York: Berkley Books, 1999.

Gray, John. *Mars and Venus in the Workplace.* New York: HarperCollins, 2002.

Hagel, John III, and Marc Singer. *Net Worth: Shaping Markets When Customers Make the Rules.* Boston: Harvard Business School Press, 1999.

Hinds, Karen S. *Get Along Get Ahead: 101 Courtesies for the New Workplace.* Boston: New Books Publishing, 2000.

Issacs, Florence. *Business Notes: Writing Personal Notes That Build Professional Relationships.* New York: Clarkson N. Potter/Publishers, 1998.

Karen, Robert. "Shame." *Atlantic Monthly,* vol. 269, no. 2 (February 1992): 40–70.

Kipfer, Barbara Ann. *14,000 Things to Be Happy About.* New York: Workman Publishing, 1990.

Linver, Sandy. *Speak Easy: How to Talk Your Way to the Top.* New York: Summit Books, 1978.

Linver, Sandy, and Jim Mengert. *Speak and Get Results.* New York: Fireside, 1994.

Lundun, Stephen C., et al. *Fish Tales.* New York: Hyperion, 2002.

Masciarelli, James P. *Power Skills: Building Top-Level Relationships for Bottom-Line Results.* Gloucester, Mass.: Nimbus Press, 2000.

McGinty, Sarah Myers. *Power Talk: Using Language to Build Authority and Influence.* New York: Warner Books, 2001.

Misner, Ivan R. *The World's Best Known Marketing Secret.* Austin, Tex.: Bard Press, 2000.

———. and Robert Davis. *Business by Referral: A Sure-Fire Way to Generate New Business.* Austin, Tex.: Bard Press, 1998.

———. and Don Morgan. *Masters of Networking.* Austin, Tex.: Bard Press, 2000.

Morgenstern, Julie. *Organizing from the Inside Out: The Foolproof System for Organizing Your Home, Your Office, and Your Life.* New York: Henry Holt, 1998.

Mundis, Jerrold. *Earn What You Deserve.* New York: Bantam Books, 1996.

Naisbitt, John. *Megatrends: Ten New Directions Transforming Our Lives.* New York: Warner Books, 1982.

Niven, David. *The 100 Simple Secrets of Happy People.* San Francisco: Harper, 2000.

Orman, Suze. *The Courage to Be Rich.* New York: Riverhead Books, 2002.

Peck, Scott. *The Love You Deserve: 10 Keys to Perfect Love.* Solana Beach, California: Lifepath Publishing, 1998.

Peters, Tom. *Reinventing Work: The Brand You 50*. New York: Borzoi, 1999.

Peters, Tom. *Reinventing Work: The Professional Service Firm 50*. New York: Borzoi, 1999.

Peters, Tom. *Reinventing Work: The Project 50*. New York: Borzoi, 1999.

Post, Peggy, and Peter Post. *The Etiquette Advantage in Business: Personal Skills for Professional Success*. New York: Harper Resource, 1999.

Ribbens, Geoff, and Richard Thompson. *Understanding Body Language*. Hong Kong: Barron's Educational Series, Inc., 2001.

Richardson, Cherryl. *Take Time for Your Life*. New York: Broadway Books, 1998.

RoAne, Susan. *The Secrets of Savvy Networking*. New York: Warner Books, 1993.

Sandler, David H. *You Can't Teach a Kid to Ride a Bike at a Seminar.* Stevenson, Maryland: Bayhead Publishing, Inc., 1999.

Schenkel, Susan. *Giving Away Success: Why Women Get Stuck and What to Do about It*. New York: Harper Perennial, 1991.

Schmidt, Peggy J. *Making It on Your First Job: When You're Young, Inexperienced and Ambitious*. New York: Avon Books, 1981.

Seligman, Martin E. P. *Learned Optimism*. New York: Pocket Books, 1998.

Sinetar, Marsha. *Do What You Love, the Money Will Follow: Discovering Your Right Livelihood*. New York: Dell Publishing, 1987.

Stanley, Thomas J. *Networking with the Affluent and Their Advisors*. New York: McGraw-Hill, 1993.

Stanny, Barbara. *Prince Charming Isn't Coming: How Women Get Smart About Money*. New York: Viking, 1997.

Stephens, Nancy J., and Bob Adams. *Customer Focused Selling*. Holbrook, Mass.: Adams Media Corporation, 1998.

Weber, Larry. *The Provacateur.* New York: Crown Business, 2001.

Whiteley, Richard C. *Love the Work You're With.* New York: Henry Holt and Company, 2001.

Index

ABOUT THE AUTHOR

Diane Darling is founder and CEO of Effective Networking, Inc., a Boston-based company that teaches professional networking techniques. She has appeared on "NBC Nightly News" and has been featured in the *Wall Street Journal*.